THE AMERICAN FRUGAL
HOUSEWIFE

BY

LYDIA MARIA CHILD

British Library Cataloguing-in-Publication Data
A catalogue record for this book is available from the
British Library

Contents

Lydia Maria Child

Lydia Maria Francis Child was born on 11th February 1802, in Medford, Massachusetts, USA. She received her early education at a local dame school and later at a women's seminary, before moving to Maine following the death of her mother. At Maine, Child studied to be a teacher and found an interest in classic literature, particularly for literary masters such as Homer and Milton to whom she was introduced by her brother, Convers, a Unitarian minister. Despite Convers' reservations, Child wrote her first novel, entitled *Hobomok* and finished it in six weeks. From here on in, she wrote continually.

Child taught for one year in a seminary in Medford, and started a private school in Watertown in 1824. Two years later, she began the publication of the *Juvenile Miscellany*, the first monthly periodical for children issued in the USA, and supervised it for eight years. In 1828, Child married the Boston lawyer David Lee Child, who was a political activist and heavily involved in the restructurings of Indian rights and Garrisonian abolitionism. Together the couple moved to Massachusetts and enjoyed a happy marriage, both unceasingly working towards the causes of individual liberties and social reform. It was only in the 1830s that Child became involved in abolitionism and women's rights

1

movements though; she came to believe that the two causes were inextricably intertwined, and no progress could be made in one without the other. Essentially, Child highlighted the fact that white men held both groups in subjugation and treated them as property instead of human beings. In 1833, her book, *An Appeal in Favour of that Class of Americans Called Africans* was published, arguing for the immediate emancipation of slaves without compensation to slaveholders. Child is credited with being the first white person to have written a book in support of this policy, and she followed it up with several smaller works on the same subject. The following year (1834) child also helped with fundraising efforts to finance the first anti-slavery fair, which was held in Boston, and in 1839 was elected to the executive committee of the American Anti-Slavery Society (AASS). She became editor of the society's *National Anti-Slavery Standard* in 1840. During this time, Child also wrote short fictional stories, elucidating the complex issues surrounding slavery; most notably, *The Quadroons* (1842) and *Slavery's Pleasant Homes: A Faithful Sketch* (1843). In the mid-1840s, Child made the decision to leave the AASS, as she refused to promote violence as an acceptable weapon for battling slavery. She also disliked the internal politics of the organisation, and ceased publically campaigning for women's rights or abolitionism. However, this changed in 1850s, with the near-fatal beating of her good friend, abolitionist Senator Charles Summer, by a fellow congressman in Kansas. Child responded to this incident by writing a poem entitled the *Kansas Emigrants* and thereafter acknowledged the need for the use of violence to protect antislavery emigrants in Kansas.

Later in life, Child also became involved in Indian rights work. Her first novel, *Hobomok: A Tale of Early Times,* told the tale of a relationship between a white woman and Native American man, with whom she had a son. The heroine later remarried however, and reintegrated herself into Puritan society. The book caused scandal in the literary community, and was not a critical success. Undeterred by the bigotry of the time, Child wrote many subsequent pamphlets on Indian rights, including *An Appeal for the Indians* (1868) which led to the founding of the U.S. Board of Indian Commissioners and the subsequent Peace Policy in the administration of Ulysses S. Grant.

After a long and full life, Child died in Wayland, Massachusetts, on 20th October 1880, aged seventy-eight. She is buried at North Cemetery in Wayland.

THE AMERICAN FRUGAL HOUSEWIFE.
DEDICATED TO
THOSE WHO ARE NOT ASHAMED OF ECONOMY.
BY MRS. CHILD,
AUTHOR OF "HOBOMOK," "THE MOTHER'S
BOOK," EDITOR OF THE "JUVENILE
MISCELLANY," &c.
A fat kitchen maketh a lean will.—FRANKLIN.
"Economy is a poor man's revenue; extravagance a rich
man's ruin."

MUTTON.

1. Leg.
2. Loin, best end.
3. Do. Chump do.
4. Neck, best do.
5. Do Scrag do.
6. Shoulder.
7. Breast.
Saddle, 2 Loins.

PORK

1. The Sperib.
2. Hand.
3. Belly, or Spring.
4. Fore Loin.
5. Hind do.
6. Leg.

VEAL

1. Loin, best end
2. Do Chump do
3. Fillet.
4. Knuckle, hind.
5. Do. fore.
6. Neck, best end.
7. Do. scrag do.
8. Blade Bone.
9. Breast, best end.
10. Do. Brisket.

BEEF

Hind Quarter.

1. Sir Loin.
2. Rump.
3. Aitch Bone.
4. Buttock.
5. Mouse do.
6. Veiny piece.
7. Thick Flank.
8. Thin do.
9. Leg.

Fore Quarter.

10. Fore Rib, 5 Ribs.
11. Middle do 4 do.
12. Chuck, 3 do.
13. Shoulder, or Leg Mutton piece.
14. Brisket.
15. Clod.
16. Neck, or Sticking piece.
17. Shin.
18. Cheek.

INTRODUCTORY CHAPTER

The true economy of housekeeping is simply the art of gathering up all the fragments, so that nothing be lost. I mean fragments of *time*, as well as *materials*. Nothing should be thrown away so long as it is possible to make any use of it, however trifling that use may be; and whatever be the size of a family, every member should be employed either in earning or saving money.

'Time is money.' For this reason, cheap as stockings are, it is good economy to knit them. Cotton and woollen yarn are both cheap; hose that are knit wear twice as long as woven ones; and they can be done at odd minutes of time, which would not be otherwise employed. Where there are children, or aged people, it is sufficient to recommend knitting, that it is an *employment*.

In this point of view, patchwork is good economy. It is indeed a foolish waste of time to tear cloth into bits for the sake of arranging it anew in fantastic figures; but a large family may be kept out of idleness, and a few shillings saved, by thus using scraps of gowns, curtains, &c.

In the country, where grain is raised, it is a good plan to teach children to prepare and braid straw for their own bonnets, and their brothers' hats.

Where turkeys and geese are kept, handsome feather fans may as well be made by the younger members of a family, as to be bought. The sooner children are taught to turn their faculties to some account, the better for them and for their parents.

In this country, we are apt to let children romp away their existence, till they get to be thirteen or fourteen. This is not well. It is not well for the purses and patience of parents; and it has a still worse effect on the morals and habits of the children. *Begin early* is the great maxim for everything in education. A child of six years old can be made useful; and should be taught to consider every day lost in which some little thing has not been done to assist others.

Children can very early be taught to take all the care of their own clothes.

They can knit garters, suspenders, and stockings; they can make patchwork and braid straw; they can make mats for the table, and mats for the floor; they can weed the garden, and pick cranberries from the meadow, to be carried to market.

Provided brothers and sisters go together, and are not allowed to go with bad children, it is a great deal better for the boys and girls on a farm to be picking blackberries at six cents a quart, than to be wearing out their clothes in useless play. They enjoy themselves just as well; and they are earning

12

something to buy clothes, at the same time they are tearing them.

It is wise to keep an exact account of all you expend—even of a paper of pins. This answers two purposes; it makes you more careful in spending money, and it enables your husband to judge precisely whether his family live within his income. No false pride, or foolish ambition to appear as well as others, should ever induce a person to live one cent beyond the income of which he is certain. If you have two dollars a day, let nothing but sickness induce you to spend more than nine shillings; if you have one dollar a day, do not spend but seventy-five cents; if you have half a dollar a day, be satisfied to spend forty cents.

To associate with influential and genteel people with an appearance of equality, unquestionably has its advantages; particularly where there is a family of sons and daughters just coming upon the theatre of life; but, like all other external advantages, these have their proper price, and may be bought too dearly. They who never reserve a cent of their income, with which to meet any unforeseen calamity, 'pay too dear for the whistle,' whatever temporary benefits they may derive from society. Self-denial, in proportion to the narrowness of your income, will eventually be the happiest and most respectable course for you and yours. If you are prosperous, perseverance and industry will not fail to place you in such a situation as your ambition covets; and if you are not prosperous, it will be well for your children that they have not been educated to higher hopes than they will ever realize.

If you are about to furnish a house, do not spend all your money, be it much or little. Do not let the beauty of this thing, and the cheapness of that, tempt you to buy unnecessary articles. Doctor Franklin's maxim was a wise one, 'Nothing is cheap that we do not want.' Buy merely enough to get along with at first. It is only by experience that you can tell what will be the wants of your family. If you spend all your money, you will find you have purchased many things you do not want, and have no means left to get many things which you do want. If you have enough, and more than enough, to get everything suitable to your situation, do not think you must spend it all, merely because you happen to have it. Begin humbly. As riches increase, it is easy and pleasant to increase in hospitality and splendour; but it is always painful and inconvenient to decrease. After all, these things are viewed in their proper light by the truly judicious and respectable. Neatness, tastefulness, and good sense, may be shown in the management of a small household, and the arrangement of a little furniture, as well as upon a larger scale; and these qualities are always praised, and always treated with respect and attention. The consideration which many purchase by living beyond their income, and of course living upon others, is not worth the trouble it costs. The glare there is about this false and wicked parade is deceptive; it does not in fact procure a man valuable friends, or extensive influence. More than that, it is wrong—morally wrong, so far as the individual is concerned; and injurious beyond calculation to the interests of our country. To what are the increasing beggary and discouraged exertions of the present period owing? A multitude of causes have no doubt tended to increase the evil; but the root of the whole matter is the extravagance of all classes of people. We never shall be prosperous till we make pride and vanity yield to the dictates of honesty and prudence! We never shall be free from embarrassment until we cease to be ashamed of industry and economy. Let women do their share towards reformation— Let their fathers and husbands see them happy without finery; and if their husbands and fathers have (as is often the case) a foolish pride in seeing them decorated, let them gently and gradually check this feeling, by showing that they have better and surer means of commanding respect—Let them prove, by the exertion of ingenuity and economy, that neatness, good taste, and gentility, are attainable without great expense.

The writer has no apology to offer for this cheap little book of economical hints, except her deep conviction that such a book is needed. In this case, renown is out of the question, and ridicule is a matter of indifference.

The information conveyed is of a common kind; but it is such as the majority of young housekeepers do not possess, and such as they cannot obtain from cookery books. Books of this kind have usually been written for the wealthy: I have written for the poor. I have said nothing about *rich* cooking; those who can afford to be epicures will find the best of information in the 'Seventy-five Receipts.' I have attempted to teach how money can be *saved*, not how it can be *enjoyed*. If any persons think some of the maxims too rigidly economical, let them inquire how the largest fortunes among us have been made. They will find thousands and millions have been accumulated by a scrupulous attention to sums 'infinitely more minute than sixty cents.'

In early childhood, you lay the foundation of poverty or riches, in the habits you give your children. Teach them to save everything,—not for their *own* use, for that would make them selfish—but for *some* use. Teach them to *share* everything with their playmates; but never allow them to *destroy* anything.

I once visited a family where the most exact economy was observed; yet nothing was mean or uncomfortable. It is the character of true economy to be as comfortable and genteel with a little, as others can be with much. In this family, when the father brought home a package, the older children would, of their own accord, put away the paper and twine neatly, instead of throwing them in the fire, or tearing

16

them to pieces. If the little ones wanted a piece of twine to play scratch-cradle, or spin a top, there it was, in readiness; and when they threw it upon the floor, the older children had no need to be told to put it again in its place.

The other day, I heard a mechanic say, 'I have a wife and two little children; we live in a very small house; but, to save my life, I cannot spend less than twelve hundred a year.' Another replied, 'You are not economical; I spend but eight hundred.' I thought to myself,—'Neither of you pick up your twine and paper.' A third one, who was present, was silent; but after they were gone, he said, 'I keep house, and comfortably too, with a wife and children, for six hundred a year; but I suppose they would have thought me mean, if I had told them so.' I did not think him mean; it merely occurred to me that his wife and children were in the habit of picking up paper and twine.

Economy is generally despised as a low virtue, tending to make people ungenerous and selfish. This is true of avarice; but it is not so of economy. The man who is economical, is laying up for himself the permanent power of being useful and generous. He who thoughtlessly gives away ten dollars, when he owes a hundred more than he can pay, deserves no praise,—he obeys a sudden impulse, more like instinct than reason: it would be real charity to check this feeling; because the good he does maybe doubtful, while the injury he does his family and creditors is certain. True economy is a careful

ODD SCRAPS
FOR THE ECONOMICAL.

If you would avoid waste in your family, attend to the following rules, and do not despise them because they appear so unimportant: 'many a little makes a mickle.'

Look frequently to the pails, to see that nothing is thrown to the pigs which should have been in the grease-pot.

Look to the grease-pot, and see that nothing is there which might have served to nourish your own family, or a poorer one.

See that the beef and pork are always *under* brine; and that the brine is sweet and clean.

Count towels, sheets, spoons, &c. occasionally; that those who use them may not become careless.

See that the vegetables are neither sprouting nor decaying: if they are so, remove them to a drier place, and spread them.

Examine preserves, to see that they are not contracting mould; and your pickles, to see that they are not growing soft and tasteless.

As far as it is possible, have bits of bread eaten up before they become hard. Spread those that are not eaten, and let them dry, to be pounded for puddings, or soaked for brewis.

Brewis is made of crusts and dry pieces of bread, soaked a good while in hot milk, mashed up, and salted, and buttered like toast. Above all, do not let crusts accumulate in such quantities that they cannot be used. With proper care, there is no need of losing a particle of bread, even in the hottest weather.

Attend to all the mending in the house, once a week, if possible. Never put out sewing. If it be impossible to do it in your own family, hire some one into the house, and work with them.

Make your own bread and cake. Some people think it is just as cheap to buy of the baker and confectioner; but it is not half as cheap. True, it is more convenient; and therefore the rich are justifiable in employing them; but those who are under the necessity of being economical, should make convenience a secondary object. In the first place, confectioners make their cake richer than people of moderate income can afford to make it; in the next place, your domestic, or yourself, may just as well employ your own time, as to pay them for theirs.

When ivory-handled knives turn yellow, rub them with nice sand paper, or emery; it will take off the spots, and restore their whiteness.

When a carpet is faded, I have been told that it may be restored, in a great measure, (provided there be no grease in it,) by being dipped into strong salt and water. I never tried this; but I know that silk pocket handkerchiefs, and deep blue factory cotton will not fade, if dipped in salt and water while new.

An ox's gall will set any color,—silk, cotton, or woollen. I have seen the colors of calico, which faded at one washing, fixed by it. Where one lives near a slaughterhouse, it is worth while to buy cheap, fading goods, and set them in this way. The gall can be bought for a few cents. Get out all the liquid, and cork it up in a large phial. One large spoonful of this in a gallon of warm water is sufficient. This is likewise excellent for taking out spots from bombazine, bombazet, &c. After being washed in this, they look about as well as when new. It must be thoroughly stirred into the water, and not put upon the cloth. It is used without soap. After being washed in this, cloth which you want to *clean* should be washed in warm suds, without using soap.

Tortoise shell and horn combs last much longer for having oil rubbed into them once in a while.

Indian meal and rye meal are in danger of fermenting in summer; particularly Indian. They should be kept in a cool place, and stirred open to the air, once in a while. A large stone, put in the middle of a barrel of meal, is a good thing to keep it cool.

The covering of oil-flasks, sewed together with strong thread, and lined and bound neatly, makes useful tablemats.

21

A warming-pan full of coals, or a shovel of coals, held over varnished furniture, will take out white spots. Care should be taken not to hold the coals near enough to scorch; and the place should be rubbed with flannel while warm.

Spots in furniture may usually be cleansed by rubbing them quick and hard, with a flannel wet with the same thing which took out the color; if rum, wet the cloth with rum, &c. The very best restorative for defaced varnished furniture, is rotten-stone pulverized, and rubbed on with linseed oil.

Sal-volatile, or hartshorn, will restore colors taken out by acid. It may be dropped upon any garment without doing harm.

Spirits of turpentine is good to take grease-spots out of woollen clothes; to take spots of paint, &c., from mahogany furniture; and to cleanse white kid gloves. Cockroaches, and all vermin, have an aversion to spirits of turpentine.

An ounce of quicksilver, beat up with the white of two eggs, and put on with a feather, is the cleanest and surest bed-bug poison. What is left should be thrown away: it is dangerous to have it about the house. If the vermin are in your walls, fill up the cracks with *verdigris*-green paint.[1]

Lamps will have a less disagreeable smell if you dip your wick-yarn in strong hot vinegar, and dry it.

Those who make candles will find it a great improvement to steep the wicks in lime-water and saltpetre, and dry them. The flame is clearer, and the tallow will not '*run*.'

Britannia Ware should be first rubbed gently with a woollen cloth and sweet oil; then washed in warm suds, and rubbed with soft leather and whiting. Thus treated, it will retain its beauty to the last.

Eggs will keep almost any length of time in lime-water properly prepared. One pint of coarse salt, and one pint of unslacked lime, to a pailful of water. If there be too much lime, it will eat the shells from the eggs; and if there be a single egg cracked, it will spoil the whole. They should be covered with lime-water, and kept in a cold place. The yolk becomes slightly red; but I have seen eggs, thus kept, perfectly sweet and fresh at the end of three years. The cheapest time to lay down eggs, is early in spring, and the middle and last of September. It is bad economy to buy eggs by the dozen, as you want them.

New iron should be very gradually heated at first. After it has become inured to the heat, it is not as likely to crack.

It is a good plan to put new earthen ware into cold water, and let it heat gradually, until it boils,—then cool again. Brown earthen ware, in particular, may be toughened in this way. A handful of rye, or wheat, bran, thrown in while it is boiling, will preserve the glazing, so that it will not be destroyed by acid or salt.

Clean a brass kettle, before using it for cooking, with salt and vinegar.

Skim-milk and water, with a bit of glue in it, heated scalding hot, is excellent to restore old, rusty, black Italian crape. If clapped and pulled dry, like nice muslin, it will look as well, or better, than when new.

Wash-leather gloves should be washed in clean suds, scarcely warm.

The oftener carpets are shaken, the longer they wear; the dirt that collects under them, grinds out the threads.

Do not have carpets swept any oftener than is absolutely necessary. After dinner, sweep the crumbs into a dusting-pan with your hearth-brush; and if you have been sewing, pick up the shreds by hand. A carpet can be kept very neat in this way; and a broom wears it very much.

Buy your woollen yarn in quantities from some one in the country, whom you can trust. The thread-stores make profits upon it, of course.

It is not well to clean brass andirons, handles, &c. with vinegar. It makes them very clean at first; but they soon spot and tarnish. Rotten-stone and oil are proper materials for cleaning brasses. If wiped every morning with flannel and New England rum, they will not need to be cleaned half as often.

If you happen to live in a house which has marble fire-places, never wash them with suds; this destroys the polish, in time. They should be dusted; the spots taken off with a nice oiled cloth, and then rubbed dry with a soft rag.

Feathers should be very thoroughly dried before they are used. For this reason they should not be packed away in bags, when they are first plucked. They should be laid lightly in a basket, or something of that kind, and stirred up often. The garret is the best place to dry them; because they will there be kept free from dirt and moisture; and will be in no danger of being blown away. It is well to put the parcels, which you may have from time to time, into the oven, after you have removed your bread, and let them stand a day.

If feather-beds smell badly, or become heavy, from want of proper preservation of the feathers, or from old age, empty them, and wash the feathers thoroughly in a tub of suds; spread them in your garret to dry, and they will be as light and as good as new.

New England rum, constantly used to wash the hair, keeps it very clean, and free from disease, and promotes its growth a great deal more than Macassar oil. Brandy is very strengthening to the roots of the hair; but it has a hot, drying tendency, which N.E. rum has not.

If you wish to preserve fine teeth, always clean them thoroughly after you have eaten your last meal at night.

Rags should never be thrown away because they are dirty. Mop-rags, lamp-rags, &c. should be washed, dried, and put in the rag-bag. There is no need of expending soap upon them: boil them out in dirty suds, after you have done washing.

Linen rags should be carefully saved; for they are extremely useful in sickness. If they have become dirty and worn by cleaning silver, &c., wash them, and scrape them into lint.

After old coats, pantaloons, &c. have been cut up for boys, and are no longer capable of being converted into garments, cut them into strips, and employ the leisure moments of children, or domestics, in sewing and braiding them for door-mats.

If you are troubled to get soft water for washing, fill a tub or barrel half full of ashes, and fill it up with water, so that you may have lye whenever you want it. A gallon of strong lye put into a great kettle of hard water will make it as soft as rain water. Some people use pearlash, or potash; but this costs something, and is very apt to injure the texture of the cloth.

If you have a strip of land, do not throw away suds. Both ashes and suds are good manure for bushes and young plants.

When a white Navarino bonnet becomes soiled, rip it in pieces, and wash it with a sponge and soft water. While it is yet damp, wash it two or three times with a clean sponge dipped into a strong saffron tea, nicely strained. Repeat this till the bonnet is as dark a straw color as you wish. Press it on the wrong side with a warm iron, and it will look like a new Leghorn.

About the last of May, or the first of June, the little millers, which lay moth-eggs begin to appear. Therefore brush all your woollens, and pack them away in a dark place covered with linen. Pepper, red-cedar chips, tobacco,— indeed, almost any strong spicy smell,—is good to keep moths out of your chests and drawers. But nothing is so good as camphor. Sprinkle your woollens with camphorated spirit, and scatter pieces of camphor-gum among them, and you will never be troubled with moths. Some people buy camphor-wood trunks, for this purpose; but they are very expensive, and the gum answers just as well.

The first young leaves of the common currant-bush, gathered as soon as they put out, and dried on tin, can hardly be distinguished from green tea.

Cream of tartar, rubbed upon soiled white kid gloves, cleanses them very much.

Bottles that have been used for rose-water, should be used for nothing else; if scalded ever so much, they will kill the spirit of what is put in them.

If you have a greater quantity of cheeses in the house than is likely to be soon used, cover them carefully with paper, fastened on with flour paste, so as to exclude the air. In this way they may be kept free from insects for years. They should be kept in a dry, cool place.

Pulverized alum possesses the property of purifying water. A large spoonful stirred into a hogshead of water will so purify it, that in a few hours the dirt will all sink to the bottom, and it will be as fresh and clear as spring water. Four gallons may be purified by a tea-spoonful.

Save vials and bottles. Apothecaries and grocers will give something for them. If the bottles are of good thick glass, they will always be useful for bottling cider or beer; but if they are thin French glass, like claret bottles, they will not answer.

Woollens should be washed in very hot suds, and not rinsed. Lukewarm water shrinks them.

On the contrary, silk, or anything that has silk in it, should be washed in water almost cold. Hot water turns it yellow. It may be washed in suds made of nice white soap; but no soap should be put upon it. Likewise avoid the use of hot irons in smoothing silk. Either rub the articles dry with a soft cloth, or put them between two towels, and press them with weights.

Do not let knives be dropped into hot dish-water. It is a good plan to have a large tin pot to wash them in, just high enough to wash the blades, *without wetting* the handles. Keep your castors covered with blotting-paper and green flannel. Keep your salt-spoons out of the salt, and clean them often.

Do not wrap knives and forks in woollens. Wrap them in good, strong paper. Steel is injured by lying in woollens.

If it be practicable, get a friend in the country to procure you a quantity of lard, butter, and eggs, at the time they are cheapest, to be put down for winter use. You will be likely to get them cheaper and better than in the city market; but by all means put down your winter's stock. Lard requires no other care than to be kept in a dry, cool place. Butter is sweetest in September and June; because food is then plenty, and not rendered bitter by frost. Pack your butter in a clean, scalded firkin, cover it with strong brine, and spread a cloth all over the top, and it will keep good until the Jews get into Grand Isle. If you happen to have a bit of salt-petre, dissolve it with the brine. Dairy-women say that butter comes more easily, and has a peculiar hardness and sweetness, if the cream is scalded and strained before it is used. The cream should stand down cellar over night, after being scalded, that it may get perfectly cold.

Suet and lard keep better in tin than in earthen.

Suet keeps good all the year round, if chopped and packed down in a stone jar, covered with molasses.

Pick suet free from veins and skin, melt it in water before a moderate fire, let it cool till it forms into a hard cake, then wipe it dry, and put it in clean paper in linen bags.

Preserve the backs of old letters to write upon. If you have children who are learning to write, buy coarse white paper by the quantity, and keep it locked up, ready to be made into writing books. It does not cost half as much as it does to buy them at the stationer's.

Do not let coffee and tea stand in tin. Scald your wooden ware often; and keep your tin ware dry.

When mattresses get hard and bunchy, rip them, take the hair out, pull it thoroughly by hand, let it lie a day or two to air, wash the tick, lay it in as light and even as possible, and catch it down, as before. Thus prepared, they will be as good as new.

It is poor economy to buy vinegar by the gallon, Buy a barrel, or half a barrel, of really strong vinegar, when you begin house-keeping. As you use it, fill the barrel with old cider, sour beer, or wine-settlings, &c., left in pitchers, decanters or tumblers; weak tea is likewise said to be good: nothing is hurtful, which has a tolerable portion of spirit, or acidity. Care must be taken not to add these things in too large quantities, or too often: if the vinegar once gets weak, it is difficult to restore it. If possible, it is well to keep such slops as I have mentioned in a different keg, and draw them off once in three or four weeks, in such a quantity as you think the vinegar will bear. If by any carelessness you do weaken it, a few white beans dropped in, or white paper dipped in molasses, is said to be useful. If beer grows sour, it may be used to advantage for pancakes and fritters. If very sour indeed, put a pint of molasses and water to it, and, two or three days after, put a half pint of vinegar; and in ten days it will be first rate vinegar.

Barley straw is the best for beds; dry corn husks, slit into shreds, are far better than straw.

Straw beds are much better for being boxed at the sides; in the same manner upholsterers prepare ticks for feathers. Brass andirons should be cleaned, done up in papers, and put in a dry place, during the summer season.

If you have a large family, it is well to keep white rags separate from colored ones, and cotton separate from woollen; they bring a higher price. Paper brings a cent a pound, and if you have plenty of room, it is well to save it. 'A penny saved is a penny got.'

Always have plenty of dish-water, and have it hot. There is no need of asking the character of a domestic, if you have ever seen her wash dishes in a little greasy water. When molasses is used in cooking, it is a prodigious improvement to boil and skim it before you use it. It takes out the unpleasant raw taste, and makes it almost as good as sugar. Where molasses is used much for cooking, it is well to prepare one or two gallons in this way at a time.

In winter, always set the handle of your pump as high as possible, before you go to bed. Except in very rigid weather, this keeps the handle from freezing. When there is reason to apprehend extreme cold, do not forget to throw a rug or horse-blanket over your pump; a frozen pump is a comfortless preparation for a winter's breakfast. Never allow ashes to be taken up in wood, or put into wood. Always have

31

your tinder-box and lantern ready for use, in case of sudden alarm. Have important papers all together, where you can lay your hand on them at once, in case of fire.

Keep an old blanket and sheet on purpose for ironing, and on no account suffer any other to be used. Have plenty of holders always made, that your towels may not be burned out in such service.

Keep a coarse broom for the cellar stairs, wood-shed, yard, &c. No good housekeeper allows her carpet broom to be used for such things.

There should always be a heavy stone on the top of your pork, to keep it down. This stone is an excellent place to keep a bit of fresh meat in the summer, when you are afraid of its spoiling.

Have all the good bits of vegetables and meat collected after dinner, and minced before they are set away; that they may be in readiness to make a little savoury mince meat for supper or breakfast. Take the skins off your potatoes before they grow cold.

Vials, which have been used for medicine, should be put into cold ashes and water, boiled, and suffered to cool before they are rinsed.

If you live in the city, where it is always easy to procure provisions, be careful and not buy too much for your daily wants, while the weather is warm.

Never leave out your clothes-line over night; and see that your clothes-pins are all gathered into a basket.

Have plenty of crash towels in the kitchen; never let your white napkins be used there.

Soap your dirtiest clothes, and soak them in soft water over night.

Use hard soap to wash your clothes, and soft to wash your floors. Soft soap is so slippery, that it wastes a good deal in washing clothes.

Instead of covering up your glasses and pictures with muslin, cover the frames only with cheap, yellow cambric, neatly put on, and as near the color of the gilt as you can procure it. This looks better; leaves the glasses open for use, and the pictures for ornament; and is an effectual barrier to dust as well as flies. It can easily be re-colored with saffron tea, when it is faded.

Have a bottle full of brandy, with as large a mouth as any bottle you have, into which cut your lemon and orange peel when they are fresh and sweet. This brandy gives a delicious flavor to all sorts of pies, puddings, and cakes. Lemon is the pleasantest spice of the two; therefore they should be kept in separate bottles. It is a good plan to preserve rose-leaves in brandy. The flavor is pleasanter than rose-water; and there are few people who have the utensils for distilling. Peach leaves steeped in brandy make excellent spice for custards and puddings.

It is easy to have a supply of horse-radish all winter. Have a quantity grated, while the root is in perfection, put it in bottles, fill it with strong vinegar, and keep it corked tight.

It is thought to be a preventive to the unhealthy influence of cucumbers to cut the slices very thin, and drop each one into cold water as you cut it. A few minutes in the water takes out a large portion of the slimy matter, so injurious to health. They should be eaten with high seasoning.

Where sweet oil is much used, it is more economical to buy it by the bottle than by the flask. A bottle holds more than twice as much as a flask, and it is never double the price.

If you wish to have free-stone hearths dark, wash them with soap, and wipe them with a wet cloth; some people rub in lamp-oil, once in a while, and wash the hearth faithfully afterwards. This does very well in a large, dirty family; for the hearth looks very clean, and is not liable to show grease spots. But if you wish to preserve the beauty of a freestone hearth, buy a quantity of free-stone powder of the stone-cutter, and rub on a portion of it wet, after you have washed your hearth in hot water. When it is dry, brush it off, and it will look like new stone. Bricks can be kept clean with redding stirred up in water, and put on with a brush. Pulverized clay mixed with redding, makes a pretty rose color. Some think it is less likely to come off, if mixed with skim milk instead of water.

But black lead is far handsomer than anything else for this purpose. It looks very well mixed with water, like redding; but it gives it a glossy appearance to boil the lead in soft soap, with a little water to keep it from burning. It should be put on with a brush, in the same manner as redding; it looks nice for a long time, when done in this way.

Keep a bag for odd pieces of tape and strings; they will come in use. Keep a bag or box for old buttons, so that you may know where to go when you want one.

Run the heels of stockings faithfully; and mend thin places, as well as holes. 'A stitch in time saves nine.'

Poke-root, boiled in water and mixed with a good quantity of molasses, set about the kitchen, the pantry, &c. in large deep plates, will kill cockroaches in great numbers, and finally rid the house of them. The Indians say that poke-root boiled into a soft poultice is the cure for the bite of a snake. I have heard of a fine horse saved by it.

A little salt sprinkled in starch while it is boiling, tends to prevent it from sticking; it is likewise good to stir it with a clean spermaceti candle.

A few potatoes sliced, and boiling water poured over them, makes an excellent preparation for cleansing and stiffening old rusty black silk.

Green tea is excellent to restore rusty silk. It should be boiled in iron, nearly a cup full to three quarts. The silk should not be wrung, and should be ironed damp.

Lime pulverized, sifted through coarse muslin, and stirred up tolerably thick in white of eggs, makes a strong cement for glass and china. Plaster of Paris is still better; particularly for mending broken images of the same material. It should be stirred up by the spoonful, as it is wanted.[2]

A bit of isinglass dissolved in gin, or boiled in spirits of wine, is said to make strong cement for broken glass, china, and sea-shells.

The lemon syrup, usually sold at fifty cents a bottle, may be made much cheaper. Those who use a great quantity of it will find it worth their while to make it. Take about a pound of Havana sugar; boil it in water down to a quart; drop in the white of an egg, to clarify it; strain it; add one quarter of an oz. of tartaric acid, or citric acid; if you do not find it sour enough, after it has stood two or three days and shaken freely, add more of the acid. A few drops of the oil of lemon improves it.

If you wish to clarify sugar and water, you are about to boil, it is well to stir in the white of one egg, while cold; if put in after it boils, the egg is apt to get hardened before it can do any good.

Those who are fond of soda powders will do well to inquire at the apothecaries for the suitable acid and alkali, and buy them by the ounce, or the pound, according to the size of their families. Experience soon teaches the right proportions; and, sweetened with a little sugar or lemon syrup, it is quite as good as what one gives five times as much for, done up in papers. The case is the same with Rochelle powders.

When the stopper of a glass decanter becomes too tight, a cloth wet with hot water and applied to the neck, will cause the glass to expand, so that the stopper may be easily removed.

Glass vessels in a cylindrical form, may be cut in two, by tying around them a worsted thread, thoroughly wet with spirits of turpentine, and then setting fire to the thread. Court plaster is made of thin silk first dipped in dissolved isinglass and dried, then dipped several times in the white of egg and dried.

When plain tortoise-shell combs are defaced, the polish may be renewed by rubbing them with pulverized rotten-stone and oil. The rotten-stone should be sifted through muslin. It looks better to be rubbed on by the hand. The jewellers afterwards polish them by rubbing them with dry *rouge powder*; but sifted magnesia does just as well—and if the ladies had rouge, perhaps they would, *by mistake*, put it upon their cheeks, instead of their combs; and thereby spoil their complexions. The best way to cleanse gold is, to wash it in warm suds made of delicate soap, with ten or fifteen drops of *sal-volatile* in it. This makes jewels very brilliant.

Straw carpets should be washed in salt and water, and wiped with a dry, coarse towel. They have a strong tendency to turn yellow; and the salt prevents it. Moisture makes them decay soon; therefore they should be kept thoroughly dry.

Rye paste is more adhesive than any other paste; because that grain is very glutinous. It is much improved by adding a little pounded alum, while it is boiling. This makes it almost as strong as glue.

Red ants are among the worst plagues that can infest a house. A lady who had long been troubled with them, assured me she destroyed them in a few days, after the following manner. She placed a dish of cracked shagbarks (of which they are more fond than of anything else) in the closet. They soon gathered upon it in troops. She then put some corrosive sublimate in a cup; ordered the dish to be carried carefully to the fire, and all its contents brushed in; while she swept the few that dropped upon the shelf into the cup, and, with a feather, wet all the cracks from whence they came, with corrosive sublimate. When this had been repeated four or five times, the house was effectually cleared. Too much care cannot be taken of corrosive sublimate, especially when children are about. Many dreadful accidents have happened in consequence of carelessness. Bottles which have contained it should be broken, and buried; and cups should be boiled out in ashes and water. If kept in the house, it should be hung up high, out of reach, with POISON written upon it in large letters.

The neatest way to separate wax from honey-comb is to tie the comb up in a linen or woollen bag; place it in a kettle of cold water, and hang it over the fire. As the water heats, the wax melts, and rises to the surface, while all the impurities remain in the bag. It is well to put a few pebbles in the bag, to keep it from floating. Honey may be separated from the comb, by placing it in the hot sun, or before the fire, with two or three colanders or sieves, each finer than the other, under it.

SOAP.

In the city, I believe, it is better to exchange ashes and grease for soap; but in the country, I am certain, it is good economy to make one's own soap. If you burn wood, you can make your own lye; but the ashes of coal is not worth much. Bore small holes in the bottom of a barrel, place four bricks around, and fill the barrel with ashes. Wet the ashes well, but not enough to drop; let it soak thus three or four days; then pour a gallon of water in every hour or two, for a day or more, and let it drop into a pail or tub beneath. Keep it dripping till the color of the lye shows the strength is exhausted. If your lye is not strong enough, you must fill your barrel with fresh ashes, and let the lye run through it. Some people take a barrel without any bottom, and lay sticks and straw across to prevent the ashes from falling through. To make a barrel of soap, it will require about five or six bushels of ashes, with at least four quarts of unslacked stone lime; if slacked, doable the quantity.

When you have drawn off a part of the lye, put the lime (whether slack or not) into two or three pails of boiling water, and add it to the ashes, and let it drain through.

It is the practice of some people, in making soap, to put the lime near the bottom of the ashes when they first set it tip; but the lime becomes like mortar, and the lye does not run through, so as to get the strength of it, which is very important in making soap, as it contracts the nitrous salts which collect in ashes, and prevents the soap from *coming*, (as the saying is.) Old ashes are very apt to be impregnated with it.

Three pounds of grease should be put into a pailful of lye. The great difficulty in making soap '*come*' originates in want of judgment about the strength of the lye. One rule may be safely trusted—If your lye will bear up an egg, or a potato, so that you can see a piece of the surface as big as ninepence, it is just strong enough. If it sink below the top of the lye, it is too weak, and will never make soap; if it is buoyed up half way, the lye is too strong; and that is just as bad. A bit of quick-lime, thrown in while the lye and grease are boiling together, is of service. When the soap becomes thick and ropy, carry it down cellar in pails and empty it into a barrel.

Cold soap is less trouble, because it does not need to boil; the sun does the work of fire. The lye must be prepared and tried in the usual way. The grease must be tried out, and strained from the scraps. Two pounds of grease (instead of three) must be used to a pailful; unless the weather is very sultry, the lye should be hot when put to the grease. It should stand in the sun, and be stirred every day. If it does not begin to look like soap in the course of five or six days, add a little hot lye to it; if this does not help it, try whether

SIMPLE REMEDIES.

Cotton wool, wet with sweet oil and paregoric, relieves the ear-ache very soon.

A good quantity of old cheese is the best thing to eat, when distressed by eating too much fruit, or oppressed with any kind of food. Physicians have given it in cases of extreme danger.

Honey and milk is very good for worms; so is strong salt water; likewise powdered sage and molasses taken freely.

For a sudden attack of quincy or croup, bathe the neck with bear's grease, and pour it down the throat. A linen rag soaked in sweet oil, butter, or lard, and sprinkled with yellow Scotch snuff, is said to have performed wonderful cures in cases of croup: it should be placed where the distress is greatest. Goose-grease, or any kind of oily grease, is as good as bear's oil.

Equal parts of camphor, spirits of wine, and hartshorn, well mixed, and rubbed upon the throat, is said to be good for the croup.

Cotton wool and oil are the best things for a burn. A poultice of wheat bran, or rye bran, and vinegar, very soon takes down the inflammation occasioned by a sprain. Brown paper, wet, is healing to a bruise. Dipped in molasses, it is said to take down inflammation.

In case of any scratch, or wound, from which the lockjaw is apprehended, bathe the injured part freely with lye or pearl-ash and water.

A rind of pork bound upon a wound occasioned by a needle, pin, or nail, prevents the lock-jaw. It should be always applied. Spirits of turpentine is good to prevent the lock-jaw. Strong soft-soap, mixed with pulverized chalk, about as thick as batter, put, in a thin cloth or bag, upon the wound, is said to be a preventive to this dangerous disorder. The chalk should be kept moist, till the wound begins to discharge itself; when the patient will find relief.

If you happen to cut yourself slightly while cooking, bind on some fine salt: molasses is likewise good.

Flour boiled thoroughly in milk, so as to make quite a thick porridge, is good in cases of dysentery. A tablespoonful of W.I. rum, a table-spoonful of sugar-baker's molasses, and the same quantity of sweet oil, well simmered together, is likewise good for this disorder; the oil softens the harshness of the other ingredients.

Black or green tea, steeped in boiling milk, seasoned with nutmeg, and best of loaf sugar, is excellent for the dysentery. Cork burnt to charcoal, about as big as a hazel-nut, macerated, and put in a tea-spoonful of brandy, with a little loaf sugar and nutmeg, is very efficacious in cases of dysentery and cholera-morbus. If nutmeg be wanting, peppermint-water may be used. Flannel wet with brandy, powdered with Cayenne pepper, and laid upon the bowels, affords great relief in cases of extreme distress.

Dissolve as much table-salt in keen vinegar, as will ferment and work clear. When the foam is discharged, cork it up in a bottle, and put it away for use. A large spoonful of this, in a gill of boiling water, is very efficacious in cases of dysentery and colic.[2]

Whortleberries, commonly called huckleberries, dried, are a useful medicine for children. Made into tea, and sweetened with molasses, they are very beneficial, when the system is in a restricted state, and the digestive powers out of order.

Blackberries are extremely useful in cases of dysentery. To eat the berries is very healthy; tea made of the roots and leaves is beneficial; and a syrup made of the berries is still better. Blackberries have sometimes effected a cure when physicians despaired.

Loaf sugar and brandy relieves a sore throat; when very bad, it is good to inhale the steam of scalding hot vinegar through the tube of a tunnel. This should be tried carefully at first, lest the throat be scalded. For children, it should be allowed to cool a little.

A stocking bound on warm from the foot, at night, is good for the sore throat.

An ointment made from the common ground-worms, which boys dig to bait fishes, rubbed on with the hand, is said to be excellent, when the sinews are drawn up by any disease or accident.

A gentleman in Missouri advertises that he had an inveterate cancer upon his nose cured by a strong potash made of the lye of the ashes of red oak bark, boiled down to the consistence of molasses. The cancer was covered with this, and, about an hour after, covered with a plaster of tar. This must be removed in a few days, and, if any protuberances remain in the wound, apply more potash to them, and the plaster again, until they entirely disappear: after which heal the wound with any common soothing salve. I never knew this to be tried.

If a wound bleeds very fast, and there is no physician at hand, cover it with the scrapings of sole-leather, scraped like coarse lint. This stops blood very soon. Always have vinegar, camphor, hartshorn, or something of that kind, in readiness, as the sudden stoppage of blood almost always makes a person faint.

Balm-of-Gilead buds bottled up in N.E. rum, make the best cure in the world for fresh cuts and wounds. Every family should have a bottle of it. The buds should be gathered in a peculiar state; just when they are well swelled, ready to burst into leaves, and well covered with gum. They last but two or three days in this state.

Plantain and house-leek, boiled in cream, and strained before it is put away to cool, makes a very cooling, soothing ointment. Plantain leaves laid upon a wound are cooling and healing.

Half a spoonful of *citric acid*, (which may always be bought of the apothecaries,) stirred in half a tumbler of water, is excellent for the head-ache.

People in general think they must go abroad for vapor-baths; but a very simple one can be made at home. Place *strong* sticks across a tub of water, at the boiling point, and sit upon them, entirely enveloped in a blanket, feet and all. The steam from the water will be a vapor-bath. Some people put herbs into the water. Steam-baths are excellent for severe colds, and for some disorders in the bowels. They should not be taken without the advice of an experienced nurse, or physician. Great care should be taken not to renew the cold after; it would be doubly dangerous.

Boiled potatoes are said to cleanse the hands as well as common soap; they prevent *chops* in the winter season, and keep the skin soft and healthy.

Water-gruel, with three or four onions simmered in it, prepared with a lump of butter, pepper, and salt, eaten just before one goes to bed, is said to be a cure for a hoarse cold. A syrup made of horseradish-root and sugar is excellent for a cold.

Very strong salt and water, when frequently applied, has been known to cure wens.

The following poultice for the throat distemper, has been much approved in England:—The pulp of a roasted apple, mixed with an ounce of tobacco, the whole wet with spirits of wine, or any other high spirits, spread on a linen rag, and bound upon the throat at any period of the disorder.

Nothing is so good to take down swellings, as a soft poultice of stewed white beans, put on in a thin muslin bag, and renewed every hour or two.

The thin white skin, which comes from suet, is excellent to bind upon the feet for chilblains. Rubbing with Castile soap, and afterwards with honey, is likewise highly recommended. But, to cure the chilblains effectually, they must be attended to often, and for a long time.

Always apply diluted laudanum to fresh wounds.

A poultice of elder-blow tea and biscuit is good as a preventive to mortification. The approach of mortification is generally shown by the formation of blisters filled with *blood*; water blisters are not alarming.

Burnt alum held in the mouth is good for the canker.

The common dark-blue violet makes a slimy tea, which is excellent for the canker. Leaves and blossoms are both good. Those who have families should take some pains to dry these flowers.

When people have a sore mouth, from taking calomel, or any other cause, tea made of low-blackberry leaves is extremely beneficial.

Tea made of slippery elm is good for the piles, and for humors in the blood; to be drank plentifully. Winter evergreen[4] is considered good for all humors, particularly scrofula. Some call it rheumatism-weed; because a tea made from it is supposed to check that painful disorder.

An ointment of lard, sulphur, and cream-of-tartar, simmered together, is good for the piles.

Elixir proprietatis is a useful family medicine for all cases when the digestive powers are out of order. One ounce of saffron, one ounce of myrrh, and one ounce of aloes. Pulverize them; let the myrrh steep in half a pint of brandy, or N.E. rum, for four days; then add the saffron and aloes; let it stand in the sunshine, or in some warm place, for a fortnight; taking care to shake it well twice a day. At the end of the fortnight, fill up the bottle (a common sized one) with brandy, or N.E. rum, and let it stand a month. It costs six times as much to buy it in small quantities, as it does to make it.

The constant use of malt beer, or malt in any way, is said to be a preservative against fevers.

Black cherry-tree bark, barberry bark, mustard-seed, petty morrel-root, and horseradish, well steeped in cider, are excellent for the jaundice.

Cotton wool and oil are the best things for a burn. When children are burned, it is difficult to make them endure the application of cotton wool. I have known the inflammation of a very bad burn extracted in one night, by the constant application of brandy, vinegar, and water, mixed together. This feels cool and pleasant, and a few drops of paregoric will soon put the little sufferer to sleep. The bathing should be continued till the pain is gone.

A few drops of the oil of Cajput on cotton wool is said to be a great relief to the tooth-ache. It occasions a smart pain for a few seconds, when laid upon the defective tooth. Any apothecary will furnish it ready dropped on cotton wool, for a few cents.

A poultice made of ginger or of common chickweed, that grows about one's door in the country, has given great relief to the tooth-ache, when applied frequently to the cheek.

A spoonful of ashes stirred in cider is good to prevent sickness at the stomach. Physicians frequently order it in cases of cholera-morbus.

When a blister occasioned by a burn breaks, it is said to be a good plan to put wheat flour upon the naked flesh.

The buds of the elder bush, gathered in early spring, and simmered with new butter, or sweet lard, make a very healing and cooling ointment.

Night sweats have been cured, when more powerful remedies had failed, by fasting morning and night, and drinking cold sage tea constantly and freely.

Lard, melted and cooled five or six times in succession, by being poured each time into a fresh pail-full of water, then simmered with sliced onions, and cooled, is said, by old nurses, to make a salve, which is almost infallible in curing inflammations produced by taking cold in wounds.

Vinegar curds, made by pouring vinegar into warm milk, put on warm, and changed pretty frequently, are likewise excellent to subdue inflammation.

Chalk wet with hartshorn is a remedy for the sting of bees; so is likewise table-salt kept moist with water.

Boil castor-oil with an equal quantity of milk, sweeten it with a little sugar, stir it well, and, when cold, give it to children for drink. They will never suspect it is medicine; and will even love the taste of it.

As molasses is often given to children as a gentle physic, it will be useful to know that West India molasses is a gentle cathartic, while sugar-baker's molasses is slightly astringent.

If a fellon or run-round appears to be coming on the finger, you can do nothing better than to soak the finger thoroughly in hot lye. It will be painful, but it will cure a disorder much more painful.

Whiskey, which has had Spanish-flies in soak, is said to be good for ring-worms; but I never knew an instance of its being tried. Unless too strong, or used in great quantities, it cannot, at least, do any harm. Washing the hands frequently in warm vinegar, is good for ring-worms.

When the toe nails have a tendency to turn in, so as to be painful, the nail should always be kept scraped *very thin*, and as near the flesh as possible. As soon as the corner of the nail can be raised up out of the flesh, it should be kept from again entering, by putting a tuft of fine lint under it.

As this book may fall into the hands of those who cannot speedily obtain a physician, it is worth while to mention what is best to be done for the bite of a rattlesnake:—Cut the flesh out, around the bite, *instantly*; that the poison may not have time to circulate in the blood. If caustic is at hand, put it upon the raw flesh; if not, the next best thing is to fill the wound with salt—renewing it occasionally. Take a dose of sweet oil and spirits of turpentine, to defend the stomach. If the whole limb swell, bathe it in salt and vinegar freely. It is well to physic the system thoroughly, before returning to usual diet.

GRUEL.

Gruel is very easily made. Have a pint of water boiling in a skillet; stir up three or four large spoonfuls of nicely sifted oat-meal, rye, or Indian, in cold water. Pour it into the skillet while the water boils. Let it boil eight or ten minutes. Throw in a large handful of raisins to boil, if the patient is well enough to bear them. When put in a bowl, add a little salt, white sugar, and nutmeg.

EGG GRUEL.

This is at once food and medicine. Some people have very great faith in its efficacy in cases of chronic dysentery. It is made thus: Boil a pint of new milk; beat four new-laid eggs to a light froth, and pour in while the milk boils; stir them together thoroughly, but do not let them boil; sweeten it with the best of loaf sugar, and grate in a whole nutmeg; add a little salt, if you like it. Drink half of it while it is warm, and the other half in two hours.

ARROW-ROOT JELLY.

Put about a pint of water in a skillet to boil; stir up a large spoonful of arrow-root powder in a cup of water; pour it into the skillet while the water is boiling; let them boil together three or four minutes. Season it with nutmeg and loaf sugar. This is very light food for an invalid. When the system is in a relaxed state, two tea-spoonfuls of brandy may be put in. Milk and loaf sugar boiled, and a spoonful of fine flour, well mixed with a little cold water, poured in while the milk is boiling, is light food in cases of similar diseases.

CALF'S FOOT JELLY.

Boil four feet in a gallon of water, till it is reduced to a quart. Strain it, and let it stand, till it is quite cool. Skim off the fat, and add to the jelly one pint of wine, half a pound of sugar, the whites of six eggs, and the juice of four large lemons; boil all these materials together eight or ten minutes. Then strain into the glasses, or jars, in which you intend to keep it. Some lay a few bits of the lemon-peel at the bottom, and let it be strained upon them.

TAPIOCA JELLY.

Wash it two or three times, soak it five or six hours; simmer it in the same water with bits of fresh lemon-peel until it becomes quite clear; then put in lemon juice, wine and loaf sugar.

SAGO JELLY.

The sago should be soaked in cold water an hour, and washed thoroughly; simmered with lemon-peel and a few cloves. Add wine and loaf sugar when nearly done; and let it all boil together a few minutes.

BEEF TEA.

Beef tea, for the sick, is made by broiling a tender steak nicely, seasoning it with pepper and salt, cutting it up, and pouring water over it, not quite boiling. Put in a little water at a time, and let it stand to soak the goodness out.

WINE WHEY.

Wine whey is a cooling and safe drink in fevers. Set half a pint of sweet milk at the fire, pour in one glass of wine, and let it remain perfectly still, till it curdles; when the curds settle, strain it, and let it cool. It should not get more than blood-warm. A spoonful of rennet-water hastens the operation. Made palatable with loaf sugar and nutmeg, if the patient can bear it.

APPLE WATER.

This is given as sustenance when the stomach is too weak to bear broth, &c. It may be made thus,—Pour boiling water on roasted apples; let them stand three hours, then strain and sweeten lightly:—Or it may be made thus,—Peel and slice tart apples, add some sugar and lemon-peel; then pour some boiling water over the whole, and let it stand covered by the fire, more than an hour.

MILK PORRIDGE.

Boil new milk; stir flour thoroughly into some cold milk in a bowl, and pour it into the kettle while the milk is boiling: let it all boil six or eight minutes. Some people like it thicker than others; I should think three large spoonfuls of flour to a quart of milk was about right. It should always be seasoned with salt; and if the patient likes, loaf sugar and nutmeg may be put in. In cases of fever, little salt or spice should be put into any nourishment; but in cases of dysentery, salt and nutmeg may be used freely: in such cases too, more flour should be put in porridge, and it should be boiled very thoroughly indeed.

STEWED PRUNES.

Stew them very gently in a small quantity of water, till the stones slip out. Physicians consider them safe nourishment in fevers.

VEGETABLES.

Parsnips should be kept down cellar, covered up in sand, entirely excluded from the air. They are good only in the spring.

Cabbages put into a hole in the ground will keep well during the winter, and be hard, fresh, and sweet, in the spring. Many farmers keep potatoes in the same way.

Onions should be kept very dry, and never carried into the cellar except in severe weather, when there is danger of their freezing. By no means let them be in the cellar after March; they will sprout and spoil. Potatoes should likewise be carefully looked to in the spring, and the sprouts broken off. The cellar is the best place for them, because they are injured by wilting; but sprout them carefully, if you want to keep them. They never sprout but three times; therefore, after you have sprouted them three times, they will trouble you no more.

Squashes should never be kept down cellar when it is possible to prevent it. Dampness injures them. If intense cold makes it necessary to put them there, bring them up as soon as possible, and keep them in some dry, warm place.

Cabbages need to be boiled an hour; beets an hour and a half. The lower part of a squash should be boiled half an hour; the neck pieces fifteen or twenty minutes longer.

Parsnips should boil an hour, or an hour and a quarter, according to size. New potatoes should boil fifteen or twenty minutes; three quarters of an hour, or an hour, is not too much for large, old potatoes; common-sized ones, half an hour. In the spring, it is a good plan to cut off a slice from the seed end of potatoes before you cook them. The seed end is opposite to that which grew upon the vine; the place where the vine was broken off may be easily distinguished. By a provision of nature, the seed end becomes watery in the spring; and, unless cut off, it is apt to injure the potato. If you wish to have potatoes mealy, do not let them stop boiling for an instant; and when they are done, turn the water off, and let them steam for ten or twelve minutes over the fire. See they don't stay long enough to burn to the kettle. In Canada, they cut the skin all off, and put them in pans, to be cooked over a stove, by steam. Those who have eaten them, say they are mealy and white, looking like large snow-balls when brought upon the table.

Potatoes boiled and mashed while hot, are good to use in making short cakes and puddings; they save flour, and less shortening is necessary.

It is said that a bit of unslacked lime, about as big as a robin's egg, thrown among old, watery potatoes, while they are boiling, will tend to make them mealy. I never saw the experiment tried.

Asparagus should be boiled fifteen or twenty minutes; half an hour, if old.

Green peas should be boiled from twenty minutes to sixty, according to their age; string beans the same. Corn should be boiled from twenty minutes to forty, according to age; dandelions half an hour, or three quarters, according to age. Dandelions are very much improved by cultivation. If cut off, without injuring the root, they will spring up again, fresh and tender, till late in the season.

Beet-tops should be boiled twenty minutes; and spinage three or four minutes. Put in no green vegetables till the water boils, if you would keep all their sweetness.

When green peas have become old and yellow, they may be made tender and green by sprinkling in a pinch or two of pearlash, while they are boiling. Pearlash has the same effect upon all summer vegetables, rendered tough by being too old. If your well-water is very hard, it is always an advantage to use a little pearlash in cooking.

Tomatoes should be skinned by pouring boiling water over them. After they are skinned, they should be stewed half an hour, in tin, with a little salt, a small bit of butter, and a spoonful of water, to keep them from burning. This is a delicious vegetable. It is easily cultivated, and yields a most abundant crop. Some people pluck them green, and pickle them.

The best sort of catsup is made from tomatoes. The vegetables should be squeezed up in the hand, salt put to them, and set by for twenty-four hours. After being passed through a sieve, cloves, allspice, pepper, mace, garlic, and whole mustard-seed should be added. It should be boiled down one third, and bottled after it is cool. No liquid is necessary, as the tomatoes are very juicy. A good deal of salt and spice is necessary to keep the catsup well. It is delicious with roast meat; and a cupful adds much to the richness of soup and chowder. The garlic should be taken out before it is bottled.

Celery should be kept in the cellar, the roots covered with tan, to keep them moist.

Green squashes that are turning yellow, and striped squashes, are more uniformly sweet and mealy than any other kind.

If the tops of lettuce be cut off when it is becoming too old for use, it will grow up again fresh and tender, and may thus be kept good through the summer.

It is a good plan to boil onions in milk and water; it diminishes the strong taste of that vegetable. It is an excellent way of serving up onions, to chop them after they are boiled, and put them in a stewpan, with a little milk, butter, salt, and pepper, and let them stew about fifteen minutes. This gives them a fine flavor, and they can be served up very hot.

HERBS.

All herbs should be carefully kept from the air. Herb tea, to do any good, should be made *very strong*.

Herbs should be gathered while in blossom. If left till they have gone to seed, the strength goes into the seed. Those who have a little patch of ground, will do well to raise the most important herbs; and those who have not, will do well to get them in quantities from some friend in the country; for apothecaries make very great profit upon them.

Sage is very useful both as a medicine, for the headache—when made into tea—and for all kinds of stuffing, when dried and rubbed into powder. It should be kept tight from the air.

Summer-savory is excellent to season soup, broth, and sausages. As a medicine, it relieves the cholic. Pennyroyal and tansy are good for the same medicinal purpose.

Green wormwood bruised is excellent for a fresh wound of any kind. In winter, when wormwood is dry, it is necessary to soften it in warm vinegar, or spirit, before it is bruised, and applied to the wound.

Hyssop tea is good for sudden colds, and disorders on the lungs. It is necessary to be very careful about exposure after taking it; it is peculiarly opening to the pores.

Tea made of colt's-foot and flax-seed, sweetened with honey, is a cure for inveterate coughs. Consumptions have been prevented by it. It should be drank when going to bed; though it does good to drink it at any time. Hoarhound is useful in consumptive complaints.

Motherwort tea is very quieting to the nerves. Students, and people troubled with wakefulness, find it useful.

Thoroughwort is excellent for dyspepsy, and every disorder occasioned by indigestion. If the stomach be foul, it operates like a gentle emetic.

Sweet-balm tea is cooling when one is in a feverish state.

Catnip, particularly the blossoms, made into tea, is good to prevent a threatened fever. It produces a fine perspiration. It should be taken in bed, and the patient kept warm.

Housekeepers should always dry leaves of the burdock and horseradish. Burdocks warmed in vinegar, with the hard, stalky parts cut out, are very soothing, applied to the feet; they produce a sweet and gentle perspiration. Horseradish is more powerful. It is excellent in cases of the ague, placed on the part affected. Warmed in vinegar, and clapped.

Succory is a very valuable herb. The tea, sweetened with molasses, is good for the piles. It is a gentle and healthy physic, a preventive of dyspepsy, humors, inflammation, and all the evils resulting from a restricted state of the system.

Elder-blow tea has a similar effect. It is cool and soothing, and peculiarly efficacious either for babes or grown people, when the digestive powers are out of order.

Lungwort, maiden-hair, hyssop, elecampane and hoarhound steeped together, is an almost certain cure for a cough. A wine-glass full to be taken when going to bed.

Few people know how to keep the flavor of sweet-marjoram; the best of all herbs for broth and stuffing. It should be gathered in bud or blossom, and dried in a tin-kitchen at a moderate distance from the fire; when dry, it should be immediately rubbed, sifted, and corked up in a bottle carefully.

English-mallows steeped in milk is good for the dysentery.

CHEAP DYE-STUFFS.

A few general rules are necessary to be observed in coloring. The materials should be perfectly clean; soap should be rinsed out in soft water; the article should be entirely wetted, or it will spot; light colors should be steeped in brass, tin, or earthen; and if set at all, should be set with alum. Dark colors should be boiled in iron, and set with copperas. Too much copperas rots the thread.

The apothecaries and hatters keep a compound of vitriol and indigo, commonly called 'blue composition.' An ounce vial full may be bought for nine-pence. It colors a fine blue. It is an economical plan to use it for old silk linings, ribbons, &c. The original color should be boiled out, and the material thoroughly rinsed in soft water, so that no soap may remain in it; for soap ruins the dye. Twelve or sixteen drops of the blue composition, poured into a quart bowl full of warm soft water, stirred, (and strained, if any settlings are perceptible,) will color a great many articles. If you wish a deep blue, pour in more of the compound. Cotton must not be colored; the vitriol destroys it; if the material you wish to color has cotton threads in it, it will be ruined. After the things are thoroughly dried, they should be washed in cool suds, and dried again; this prevents any bad effects from the vitriol; if shut up from the air without being washed, there is danger of the texture being destroyed. If you wish to color green, have your cloth free as possible from the old color, clean, and rinsed, and, in the first place, color it a deep yellow. Fustic boiled in soft water makes the strongest and brightest yellow dye; but saffron, barberry bush, peach leaves, or onion skins, will answer pretty well. Next take a bowl full of strong yellow dye, and pour in a great spoonful or more of the blue composition. Stir it up well with a clean stick, and dip the articles you have already colored yellow into it, and they will take a lively grass green. This is a good plan for old bombazet curtains, dessert cloths, old flannel for covering a desk, &c; it is likewise a handsome color for ribbons.

Balm blossoms, steeped in water, color a pretty rose-color. This answers very well for the linings of children's bonnets, for ribbons, &c. It fades in the course of one season; but it is very little trouble to recolor with it. It merely requires to be steeped and strained. Perhaps a small piece of alum might serve to set the color, in some degree. In earthen or tin.

Saffron, steeped in earthen and strained, colors a fine straw color. It makes a delicate or deep shade according to the strength of the tea. The dry outside skins of onions, steeped in scalding water and strained, color a yellow very much like 'bird of paradise' color. Peach leaves, or bark scraped from the barberry bush, colors a common bright yellow. In

65

all these cases, a little piece of alum does no harm, and may help to fix the color. Ribbons, gauze handkerchiefs, &c. are colored well in this way, especially if they be stiffened by a bit of gum-Arabic, dropped in while the stuff is steeping.

The purple paper, which comes on loaf sugar, boiled in cider, or vinegar, with a small bit of alum, makes a fine purple slate color. Done in iron.

White maple bark makes a good light-brown slate color. This should be boiled in water, set with alum. The color is reckoned better when boiled in brass, instead of iron.

The purple slate and the brown slate are suitable colors for stockings; and it is an economical plan, after they have been mended and cut down, so that they will no longer look decent, to color old stockings, and make them up for children.

A pailful of lye, with a piece of copperas half as big as a hen's egg boiled in it, will color a fine nankin color, which will never wash out. This is very useful for the linings of bed-quilts, comforters, &c. Old faded gowns, colored in this way, may be made into good petticoats. Cheap cotton cloth may be colored to advantage for petticoats, and pelisses for little girls.

A very beautiful nankin color may likewise be obtained from birch-bark, set with alum. The bark should be covered with water, and boiled thoroughly in brass or tin. A bit of alum half as big as a hen's egg is sufficient. If copperas be used instead of alum, slate color will be produced.

Tea-grounds boiled in iron, and set with copperas, make a very good slate color.

Log-wood and cider, in iron, set with copperas, makes a good black. Rusty nails, or any rusty iron, boiled in vinegar, with a small bit of copperas, makes a good black,—black ink-powder done in the same way answers the same purpose.

MEAT CORNED, OR SALTED, HAMS, &C.

When you merely want to corn meat, you have nothing to do but to rub in salt plentifully, and let it set in the cellar a day or two. If you have provided more meat than you can use while it is good, it is well to corn it in season to save it. In summer, it will not keep well more than a day and a half; if you are compelled to keep it longer, be sure and rub in more salt, and keep it carefully covered from cellar-flies. In winter, there is no difficulty in keeping a piece of corned beef a fortnight or more. Some people corn meat by throwing it into their beef barrel for a few days; but this method does not make it so sweet. A little salt-petre rubbed in before you apply the common salt, makes the meat tender; but in summer it is not well to use it, because it prevents the other salt from impregnating; and the meat does not keep as well.

If you wish to salt fat pork, scald coarse salt in water and skim it, till the salt will no longer melt in the water. Pack your pork down in tight layers; salt every layer; when the brine is cool, cover the pork with it, and keep a heavy stone on the top to keep the pork under brine. Look to it once in a while, for the first few weeks, and if the salt has all melted, throw in more. This brine, scalded and skimmed every time it is used, will continue good twenty years. The rind of the pork should be packed towards the edge of the barrel.

It is good economy to salt your own beef as well as pork. Six pounds of coarse salt, eight ounces of brown sugar, a pint of molasses, and eight ounces of salt-petre, are enough to boil in four gallons of water. Skim it clean while boiling. Put it to the beef cold; have enough to cover it; and be careful your beef never floats on the top. If it does not smell perfectly sweet, throw in more salt; if a scum rises upon it, scald and skim it again, and pour it on the beef when cold.

Legs of mutton are very good, cured in the same way as ham. Six pounds of salt, eight ounces of salt-petre, and five pints of molasses, will make pickle enough for one hundred weight. Small legs should be kept in pickle twelve or fifteen days; if large, four or five weeks are not too much. They should be hung up a day or two to dry, before they are smoked. Lay them in the oven, on crossed sticks, and make a fire at the entrance. Cobs, walnut-bark, or walnut-chips, are the best to use for smoking, on account of the sweet taste they give the meat. The smallest pieces should be smoked forty-eight hours, and large legs four or five days. Some people prefer the mutton boiled as soon as it is taken from the pickle, before it is smoked; others hang it up till it gets dry thoroughly, and eat it in thin slices, like hung beef. When legs of meat are put in pickle, the thickest part of the leg should be placed uppermost, that is, standing upright, the same as the creature stood when living. The same rule should be observed when they are hung up to dry; it is essential in order to keep in the juices of the meat. Meat should be turned over once or twice during the process of smoking.

The old-fashioned way for curing hams is to rub them with salt very thoroughly, and let them lay twenty-four hours. To each ham allow two ounces of salt-petre, one quart of common salt and one quart of molasses. First baste them with molasses; next rub in the salt-petre; and, last of all, the common salt. They must be carefully turned and rubbed every day for six weeks; then hang them in a chimney, or smoke-house, four weeks.

They should be well covered up in paper bags, and put in a chest, or barrel, with layers of ashes, or charcoal, between. When you take out a ham to cut for use, be sure and put it away in a dark place, well covered up; especially in summer.

Some very experienced epicures and cooks, think the old-fashioned way of preparing bacon is troublesome and useless. They say that legs of pork placed upright in pickle, for four or five weeks, are just as nice as those rubbed with so much care. The pickle for pork and hung beef, should be stronger than for legs of mutton. Eight pounds of salt, ten ounces of salt-petre and five pints of molasses is enough for one hundred weight of meat; water enough to cover the meat well—probably, four or five gallons. Any one can prepare bacon, or dried beef, very easily, in a common oven, according to the above directions. The same pickle that answers for bacon is proper for neat's tongues. Pigs' tongues are very nice, prepared in the same way as neat's tongues; an abundance of them are sold for rein-deer's tongues, and, under that name, considered a wonderful luxury.

Neat's tongue should be boiled full three hours. If it has been in salt long, it is well to soak it over night in cold water. Put it in to boil when the water is cold. If you boil it in a small pot, it is well to change the water, when it has boiled an hour and a half; the fresh water should boil before the half-cooked tongue is put in again. It is nicer for being kept in a cool place a day or two after being boiled. Nearly the same rules apply to salt beef. A six pound piece of corned beef should boil full three hours; and salt beef should be boiled four hours.

The saltier meat is, the longer it should be boiled. If very salt, it is well to put it in soak over night; change the water while cooking; and observe the same rules as in boiling tongue. If it is intended to be eaten when cold, it is a good plan to put it between clean boards, and press it down with heavy weights for a day or two. A small leg of bacon should be boiled three hours; ten pounds four hours; twelve pounds five hours. All meat should boil moderately; furious boiling injures the flavor.

Buffalo's tongue should soak a day and a night, and boil as much as six hours.

CHOICE OF MEAT.

If people wish to be economical, they should take some pains to ascertain what are the cheapest pieces of meat to buy; not merely those which are cheapest in price, but those which go farthest when cooked. That part of mutton called the rack, which consists of the neck, and a few of the rib bones below, is cheap food. It is not more than four or five cents a pound; and four pounds will make a dinner for six people. The neck, cut into pieces, and boiled slowly an hour and a quarter, in little more than water enough to cover it, makes very nice broth. A great spoonful of rice should be washed and thrown in with the meat. About twenty minutes before it is done, put in a little thickening, and season with salt, pepper, and sifted summer-savory, or sage. The bones below the neck, broiled, make a good mutton chop. If your family be small, a rack of mutton will make you two dinners,—broth once, and mutton chop with a few slices of salt pork, for another; if your family consist of six or seven, you can have two dishes for a dinner. If you boil the whole rack for broth, there will be some left for mince meat.

Liver is usually much despised; but when well cooked, it is very palatable; and it is the cheapest of all animal food. Veal liver is by some considered the best. Veal liver is usually two cents a pound; beef liver is one cent. After you have fried a few slices of salt pork, put the liver in while the fat is very hot, and cook it through thoroughly. If you doubt whether it be done, cut into a slice, and see whether it has turned entirely brown, without any red stripe in the middle. Season it with pepper and salt, and butter, if you live on a farm, and have butter in plenty. It should not be cooked on furiously hot coals, as it is very apt to scorch. Sprinkle in a little flour, stir it, and pour in boiling water to make gravy, just as you would for fried meat. Some think liver is better dipped in sifted Indian meal before it is fried. It is good broiled and buttered like a steak. It should be cut into slices about as thick as are cut for steaks.

The heart, liver, &c. of a pig is good fried; so is that of a lamb. The latter is commonly called lamb-fry; and a dinner may be bought for six or eight cents. Be sure and ask for the sweet-bread; for butchers are extremely apt to reserve it for their own use; and therefore lamb-fry is almost always sold without it. Fry five or six slices of salt pork; after it is taken out, put in your lamb-fry while the fat is hot. Do it thoroughly; but be careful the fire is not too furious, as it is apt to scorch. Take a large handful of parsley, see that it is washed clean, cut it up pretty fine; then pour a little boiling water into the fat in which your dinner has been fried, and let the parsley cook in it a minute or two; then take it out in a spoon, and lay it over your slices of meat. Some people, who like thick gravies, shake in a little flour into the spider, before pouring in the boiling water.

Bones from which roasting pieces have been cut, may be bought in the market for ten or twelve cents, from which a very rich soup may be made, besides skimming off fat for shortening. If the bones left from the rump be bought, they will be found full of marrow, and will give more than a pint of good shortening, without injuring the richness of the soup. The richest piece of beef for a soup is the leg and the shin of beef; the leg is on the hind quarter, and the shin is on the fore quarter. The leg rand, that is, the thick part of the leg above the bony parts, is very nice for mince pies. Some people have an objection to these parts of beef, thinking they must be stringy; but, if boiled *very tender*, the sinews are not perceived, and add, in fact, to the richness of a soup.

The thick part of a thin flank is the most profitable part in the whole ox to buy. It is not so handsome in appearance as some other pieces, but it is thick meat, with very little bone, and is usually two cents less in the pound than more fashionable pieces. It is good for roasting, and particularly for corning and salting. The navel end of the brisket is one of the best pieces for salting or corning, and is very good for roasting.

The rattle rand is the very best piece for corning, or salting.

A bullock's heart is very profitable to use as a steak. Broiled just like beef. There are usually five pounds in a heart, and it can be bought for twenty-five cents. Some people stuff and roast it.

The chuck, between the neck and the shoulder, is a very good piece for roasting,—for steaks, or for salting. Indeed, it is good for almost anything; and it is cheap, being from four to five cents a pound.

The richest, tenderest, and most delicate piece of beef for roasting, or for steak, is the rump and the last cut of the sirloin. It is peculiarly appropriate for an invalid, as it is lighter food than any other beef.

But if economy be consulted instead of luxury, the round will be bought in preference to the rump. It is heartier food, and, of course, less can be eaten; and it is cheaper in price.

The shoulder of veal is the most economical for roasting or boiling. It is always cheap, let veal bear what price it may. Two dinners may be made from it; the shoulder roasted, and the knuckle cut off to be boiled with a bit of pork and greens, or to be made into soup.

The breast of veal is a favorite piece, and is sold high.

The hind-quarter of veal and the loin make two good roasting pieces. The leg is usually stuffed. The line has the kidney upon it; the fore-quarter has the brisket on it. This is a sweet and delicate morsel; for this reason some people prefer the fore-quarter to any other part.

Always buy a shoulder of pork for economy, for roasting, or coming to boil. Cut off the leg to be boiled. Many people buy the upper part of the spare-rib of pork thinking it the most genteel; but the lower part of the spare-rib toward the neck is much more sweet and juicy, and there is more meat in proportion to the bone.

The breast, or shoulder, of mutton are both nice, either for roasting, boiling or broth. The breast is richer than the shoulder. It is more economical to buy a fore-quarter of mutton than a hind-quarter; there is usually two cents difference per pound. The neck of fat mutton makes a good steak for broiling.

Lamb brings the same price, either fore-quarter or hind-quarter; therefore it is more profitable to buy a hind-quarter than a fore-quarter; especially as its own fat will cook it, and there is no need of pork or butter in addition. Either part is good for roasting or boiling. The loin of lamb is suitable for roasting, and is the most profitable for a small family. The leg is more suitable for boiling than for anything else; the shoulder and breast are peculiarly suitable for broth.

The part that in lamb is called the loin, in mutton is called the chop. Mutton chop is considered very good for broiling.

Pig's head is a profitable thing to buy. It is despised, because it is cheap; but when well cooked it is delicious. Well cleaned, the tip of the snout chopped off, and put in brine a week, it is very good for boiling: the cheeks, in particular, are very sweet; they are better than any other pieces of pork to bake with beans. The head is likewise very good baked about an hour and a half. It tastes like roast pork, and yields abundance of sweet fat, for shortening.

COMMON COOKING.

It is necessary to be very careful of fresh meat in the summer season. The moment it is brought into the house, it should be carefully covered from the flies, and put in the coldest place in the cellar. If it consist of pieces, they should be spread out separate from each other, on a large dish, and covered. If you are not to cook it soon, it is well to sprinkle salt on it. The kidney, and fat flabby parts, should be raised up above the lean, by a skewer, or stick, and a little salt strewn in. If you have to keep it over night, it should be looked to the last thing when you go to bed; and if there is danger, it should be scalded.

VEAL.

Veal should boil about an hour, if a neck-piece; if the meat comes from a thicker, more solid part, it should boil longer. No directions about these things will supply the place of judgment and experience. Both mutton and veal are better for being boiled with a small piece of salt pork. Veal broth is very good.

Veal soup should be slowly stewed for two hours. Seasoned the same as above. Some people like a little sifted summer-savory.

Six or seven pounds of veal will roast in an hour and a half.

Fried veal is better for being dipped in white of egg, and rolled in nicely pounded crumbs of bread, before it is cooked. One egg is enough for a common dinner.

CALF'S HEAD.

Calf's head should be cleansed with very great care; particularly the lights. The head, the heart, and the lights should boil full two hours; the liver should be boiled only one hour. It is better to leave the wind-pipe on, for if it hangs out of the pot while the head is cooking, all the froth will escape through it. The brains, after being thoroughly washed, should be put in a little bag; with one pounded cracker, or as much crumbled bread, seasoned with sifted sage, and tied up and boiled one hour. After the brains are boiled, they should be well broken up with a knife, and peppered, salted, and buttered. They should be put upon the table in a bowl by themselves. Boiling water, thickened with flour and water, with butter melted in it, is the proper sauce; some people love vinegar and pepper mixed with the melted butter; but all are not fond of it; and it is easy for each one to add it for themselves.

BEEF.

Beef soup should be stewed four hours over a slow fire. Just water enough to keep the meat covered. If you have any bones left of roast meat, &c. it is a good plan to boil them with the meat, and take them out half an hour before the soup is done. A pint of flour and water, with salt, pepper, twelve or sixteen onions, should be put in twenty minutes before the soup is done. Be careful and not throw in salt and pepper too plentifully; it is easy to add to it, and not easy to diminish. A lemon, cut up and put in half an hour before it is done, adds to the flavor. If you have tomato catsup in the house, a cupful will make soup rich. Some people put in crackers; some thin slices of crust, made nearly as short as common shortcake; and some stir up two or three eggs with milk and flour, and drop it in with a spoon.

A quarter of an hour to each pound of beef is considered a good rule for roasting; but this is too much when the bone is large, and the meal thin. Six pounds of the rump should roast six quarters of an hour; but bony pieces less. It should be done before a quick fire.

The quicker beef-steak can be broiled the better. Seasoned after it is taken from the gridiron.

ALAMODE BEEF.

Tie up a round of beef so as to keep it in shape; make a stuffing of grated bread, suet, sweet herbs, quarter of an ounce of nutmeg, a few cloves pounded, yolk of an egg. Cut holes in the beef, and put in the stuffing, leaving about half the stuffing to be made into balls. Tie the beef up in a cloth, just cover it with water, let it boil an hour and a half; then turn it, and let it boil an hour and a half more; then turn out the liquor, and put some skewers across the bottom of the pot, and lay the beef upon it, to brown; turn it that it may brown on both sides. Put a pint of claret, and some allspice and cloves, into the liquor, and boil some balls made of the stuffing in it.

MUTTON AND LAMB.

Six or seven pounds of mutton will roast in an hour and a half. Lamb one hour. Mutton is apt to taste strong; this may be helped by soaking the meat in a little salt and water, for an hour before cooking. However, unless meat is very sweet, it is best to corn it, and boil it.

Fresh meat should never be put in to cook till the water boils; and it should be boiled in as little water as possible; otherwise the flavor is injured. Mutton enough for a family of five or six should boil an hour and a half. A leg of lamb should boil an hour, or little more than an hour, perhaps. Put a little thickening into boiling water; strain it nicely; and put sweet butter in it for sauce. If your family like broth, throw in some clear rice when you put in the meat. The rice should be in proportion to the quantity of broth you mean to make. A large table spoonful is enough for three pints of water. Seasoned with a very little pepper and salt. Summer-savory, or sage, rubbed through a sieve, thrown in.

PORK.

Fresh pork should be cooked more than any other meat. A thick shoulder piece should be roasted full two hours and a half; and other pieces less in proportion. The slight sickness occasioned by eating roasted pork may be prevented by soaking it in salt and water the night before you cook it. If called to prepare it on short notice, it will answer to baste it with weak brine while roasting; and then turn the brine off, and throw it away.

ROAST PIG.

Strew fine salt over it an hour before it is put down. It should not be cut entirely open; fill it up plump with thick slices of buttered bread, salt, sweet-marjoram and sage. Spit it with the head next the point of the spit; take off the joints of the leg, and boil them with the liver, with a little whole pepper, allspice, and salt, for gravy sauce. The upper part of the legs must be braced down with skewers. Shake on flour. Put a little water in the dripping-pan, and stir it often. When the eyes drop out, the pig is half done. When it is nearly done, baste it with butter. Cut off the head, split it open between the eyes. Take out the brains, and chop them fine with the liver and some sweet-marjoram and sage; put this into melted butter, and when it has boiled a few minutes, add it to the gravy in the dripping-pan. When your pig is cut open, lay it with the back to the edge of the dish; half a head to be placed at each end. A good sized pig needs to be roasted three hours.

SAUSAGES.

Three tea-spoons of powdered sage, one and a half of salt, and one of pepper, to a pound of meat, is good seasoning for sausages.

MINCE MEAT.

There is a great difference in preparing mince meat. Some make it a coarse, unsavory dish; and others make it nice and palatable. No economical house-keeper will despise it; for broken bits of meat and vegetables cannot so well be disposed of in any other way. If you wish to have it nice, mash your vegetables fine, and chop your meat very fine. Warm it with what remains of sweet gravy, or roast-meat drippings, you may happen to have. Two or three apples, pared, cored, sliced, and fried, to mix with it, is an improvement. Some like a little sifted sage sprinkled in.

It is generally considered nicer to chop your meat fine, warm it in gravy, season it, and lay it upon a large slice of toasted bread to be brought upon the table without being mixed with potatoes; but if you have cold vegetables, use them.

BEANS AND PEAS.

Baked beans are a very simple dish, yet few cook them well. They should be put in cold water, and hung over the fire, the night before they are baked. In the morning, they should be put in a colander, and rinsed two or three times; then again placed in a kettle, with the pork you intend to bake, covered with water, and kept scalding hot, an hour or more. A pound of pork is quite enough for a quart of beans, and that is a large dinner for a common family. The rind of the pork should be slashed. Pieces of pork alternately fat and lean, are the most suitable; the cheeks are the best. A little pepper sprinkled among the beans, when they are placed in the bean-pot, will render them less unhealthy. They should be just covered with water, when put into the oven; and the pork should be sunk a little below the surface of the beans. Bake three or four hours.

Stewed beans are prepared in the same way. The only difference is, they are not taken out of the scalding water, but are allowed to stew in more water, with a piece of pork and a little pepper, three hours or more.

Dried peas need not be soaked over night. They should be stewed slowly four or five hours in considerable water, with a piece of pork. The older beans and peas are, the longer they should cook. Indeed, this is the case with all vegetables.

SOUSE.

Pigs' feet, ears, &c., should be cleaned after being soaked in water not very hot; the hoofs will then come off easily with a sharp knife; the hard, rough places should be cut off; they should be thoroughly singed, and then boiled as much as four or five hours, until they are too tender to be taken out with a fork. When taken from the boiling water, it should be put into cold water. After it is packed down tight, boil the jelly-like liquor in which it was cooked with an equal quantity of vinegar; salt as you think fit, and cloves, allspice, and cinnamon, at the rate of a quarter of a pound to one hundred weight: to be poured on scalding hot.

TRIPE.

Tripe should be kept in cold water, or it will become too dry for cooking. The water in which it is kept should be changed more or less frequently, according to the warmth of the weather. Broiled like a steak, buttered, peppered, &c. Some people like it prepared like souse.

GRAVY.

Most people put a half a pint of flour and water into their tin-kitchen, when they set meat down to roast. This does very well; but gravy is better flavored, and looks darker, to shake flour and salt upon the meat; let it brown thoroughly, put flour and salt on again, and then baste the meat with about half a pint of hot water (or more, according to the gravy you want.) When the meat is about done, pour these drippings into a skillet, and let it boil. If it is not thick enough, shake in a little flour; but be sure to let it boil, and be well stirred, after the flour is in. If you fear it will be too greasy, take off a cupful of the fat before you boil. The fat of beef, pork, turkeys and geese is as good for shortening as lard. Salt gravy to your taste. If you are very particular about dark gravies, keep your dredging-box full of scorched flour for that purpose.

POULTRY.

There are various ways of deciding about the age of poultry.

If the bottom of the breast bone, which extends down between the legs, is soft, and gives easily, it is a sign of youth; if stiff, the poultry is old.

If young, the legs are lighter, and the feet do not look so hard, stiff, and worn.

There is more deception in geese than in any other kind of poultry. The above remarks are applied to them; but there are other signs more infallible. In a young goose, the cavity under the wings is very tender; it is a bad sign if you cannot, with very little trouble, push your finger directly into the flesh. There is another means by which you may decide whether a goose be tender, if it be frozen or not. Pass the head of a pin along the breast, or sides, and if the goose be young, the skin will rip, like fine paper under a knife.

Something may be judged concerning the age of a goose by the thickness of the web between the toes. When young, this is tender and transparent; it grows coarser and harder with time.

In broiling chickens, it is difficult to do the inside of the thickest pieces without scorching the outside. It is a good plan to parboil them about ten minutes in a spider or skillet, covered close to keep the steam in; then put them upon the gridiron, broil and butter. It is a good plan to cover them with a plate, while on the gridiron. They may be basted with a very little of the water in which they were broiled; and if you have company who like melted butter to pour upon the chicken, the remainder of the liquor will be good use for that purpose.

An hour is enough for common sized chickens to roast. A smart fire is better than a slow one; but they must be tended closely. Slices of bread, buttered, salted, and peppered, put into the stomach (not the crop) are excellent.

Chickens should boil about an hour. If old, they should boil longer. In as little water as will cook them. Chicken-broth made like mutton-broth.

FRICASSEED CHICKEN, BROWN.

Singe the chickens; cut them in pieces; pepper, salt, and flour them; fry them in fresh butter, till they are very brown: take the chickens out, and make a good gravy, into which put sweet herbs (marjoram or sage) according to your taste; if necessary, add pepper and salt; butter and flour must be used in making the gravy, in such quantities as to suit yourself for thickness and richness. After this is all prepared, the chicken must be stewed in it, for half an hour, closely covered. A pint of gravy is about enough for two chickens; I should think a piece of butter about as big as a walnut, and a table-spoonful of flour, would be enough for the gravy. The herbs should, of course, be pounded and sifted. Some, who love onions, slice two or three, and brown them with the chicken. Some slice a half lemon, and stew with the chicken. Some add tomatoes catsup.

FRICASSEED CHICKEN, WHITE.

The chickens are cut to pieces, and covered with warm water, to draw out the blood. Then put into a stew-pan, with three quarters of a pint of water, or veal broth, salt, pepper, flour, butter, mace, sweet herbs pounded and sifted; boil it half an hour. If it is too fat, skim it a little. Just before it is done, mix the yolk of two eggs with a gill of cream, grate in a little nutmeg, stir it up till it is thick and smooth, squeeze in half a lemon. If you like onions, stew some slices with the other ingredients.

TO CURRY FOWL.

Fry out two or three slices of salt pork; cut the chicken in pieces, and lay it in the stew-pan with one sliced onion; when the fowl is tender, take it out, and put in thickening into the liquor, one spoonful of flour, and one spoonful of curry-powder, well stirred up in water. Then lay the chicken in again, and let it boil up a few minutes. A half a pint of liquor is enough for one chicken. About half an hour's stewing is necessary. The juice of half a lemon improves it; and some like a spoonful of tomatoes catsup.

CHICKEN BROTH.

Cut a chicken in quarters; put it into three or four quarts of water; put in a cup of rice while the water is cold; season it with pepper and salt; some use nutmeg. Let it stew gently, until the chicken falls apart. A little parsley, shred fine, is an improvement. Some slice up a small onion and stew with it. A few pieces of cracker may be thrown in if you like.

A common sized goose should roast full three quarters of an hour. The oil that drips from it should be nearly all turned off; it makes the gravy too greasy; and it is nice for shortening. It should first be turned into cold water; when hardened, it should be taken off and scalded in a skillet. This process leaves it as sweet as lard.

Ducks do not need to be roasted more than fifteen or twenty minutes. Butter melted in boiling flour and water is proper sauce for boiled lamb, mutton, veal, turkeys, geese, chickens, and fish. Some people cut up parsley fine, and throw in. Some people like capers put in. Others heat oysters through on the gridiron, and take them out of the shells, and throw them into the butter.

A good sized turkey should be roasted two hours and a half, or three hours; very slowly at first. If you wish to make plain stuffing, pound a cracker, or crumble some bread very fine, chop some raw salt pork very fine, sift some sage, (and summer-savory, or sweet-marjoram, if you have them in the house, and fancy them,) and mould them all together, seasoned with a little pepper. An egg worked in makes the stuffing cut better; but it is not worth while when eggs are dear. About the same length of time is required for boiling and roasting.

Pigeons may be either roasted, potted or stewed. Potting is the best, and the least trouble. After they are thoroughly picked and cleaned, put a small slice of salt pork, and a little ball of stuffing, into the body of every pigeon. The stuffing should be made of one egg to one cracker, an equal quantity of suet, or butter, seasoned with sweet-marjoram, or sage, if marjoram cannot be procured. Flour the pigeons well, lay them close together in the bottom of the pot, just cover them with water, throw in a bit of butter, and let them stew an hour and a quarter if young; an hour and three quarters if old. Some people turn off the liquor just before they are done, and brown the pigeons on the bottom of the pot; but this is very troublesome, as they are apt to break to pieces.

Stewed pigeons are cooked in nearly the same way, with the omission of the stuffing. Being dry meat, they require a good deal of butter.

91

Pigeons should be stuffed and roasted about fifteen minutes before a smart fire. Those who like birds just warmed through, would perhaps think less time necessary. It makes them nicer to butter them well just before you take them off the spit, and sprinkle them with nicely pounded bread, or cracker. All poultry should be basted and floured a few minutes before it is taken up.

The age of pigeons can be judged by the color of the legs. When young, they are of a pale delicate brown; as they grow older, the color is deeper and redder.

A nice way of serving up cold chicken, or pieces of cold fresh meat, is to make them into a meat pie. The gizzards, livers, and necks of poultry, parboiled, are good for the same purpose. If you wish to bake your meat pie, line a deep earthen or tin pan with paste made of flour, cold water, and lard; use but little lard, for the fat of the meat will shorten the crust. Lay in your bits of meat, or chicken, with two or three slices of salt pork; place a few thin slices of your paste here and there; drop in an egg or two, if you have plenty. Fill the pan with flour and water, seasoned with a little pepper and salt. If the meat be very lean, put in a piece of butter, or such sweet gravies as you may happen to have. Cover the top with crust, and put it in the oven, or bake-kettle, to cook half an hour, or an hour, according to the size of the pie. Some people think this the nicest way of cooking fresh chickens. When thus cooked, they should be parboiled before they are put into the pan, and the water they are boiled in should be added. A chicken pie needs to be cooked an hour and a half, if parboiled; two hours, if not.

If you wish to make a pot pie instead of a baked pie, you have only to line the bottom of a porridge pot with paste, lay in your meat, season and moisten it in the same way, cover it with paste, and keep it slowly stewing about the same time that the other takes. In both cases, it is well to lift the upper crust, a little while before you take up the pie, and see whether the moisture has dried away; if so, pour in flour and water well mixed, and let it boil up.

Potatoes should be boiled in a separate vessel.

If you have fear that poultry may become musty before you want to cook it, skin an onion, and put in it; a little pepper sprinkled in is good; it should be kept hung up in a dry, cool place.

If poultry is injured before you are aware of it, wash it very thoroughly in pearlash and water, and sprinkle pepper inside when you cook it. Some people hang up poultry with a muslin bag of charcoal inside. It is a good plan to singe injured poultry over lighted charcoal, and to hold a piece of lighted charcoal inside, a few minutes.

Many people parboil the liver and gizzard, and cut it up very fine, to be put into the gravy, while the fowls are cooking; in this case, the water they are boiled in should be used to make the gravy.

93

FISH.

Cod has white stripes, and a haddock black stripes; they may be known apart by this. Haddock is the best for frying; and cod is the best for boiling, or for a chowder. A thin tail is a sign of a poor fish; always choose a thick fish. When you are buying mackerel, pinch the belly to ascertain whether it is good. If it gives under your finger, like a bladder half filled with wind, the fish is poor; if it feels hard like butter, the fish is good. It is cheaper to buy one large mackerel for ninepence, than two for four pence half-penny each.

Fish should not be put in to fry until the fat is boiling hot; it is very necessary to observe this. It should be dipped in Indian meal before it is put in; and the skinny side uppermost, when first put in, to prevent its breaking. It relishes better to be fried after salt pork, than to be fried in lard alone. People are mistaken, who think fresh fish should be put into cold water as soon as it is brought into the house; soaking it in water is injurious. If you want to keep it sweet, clean it, wash it, wipe it dry with a clean towel, sprinkle salt inside and out, put it in a covered dish, and keep it on the *cellar* floor until you want to cook it. If you live remote from the seaport, and cannot get fish while hard and fresh, wet it with an egg beaten, before you meal it, to prevent its breaking.

Fish gravy is very much improved by taking out some of the fat, after the fish is fried, and putting in a little butter. The fat thus taken out will do to fry fish again; but it will not do for any kind of shortening. Shake in a little flour into the hot fat, and pour in a little boiling water; stir it up well, as it boils, a minute or so. Some people put in vinegar; but this is easily added by those who like it.

A common sized cod-fish should be put in when the water is boiling hot, and boil about twenty minutes. Haddock is not as good for boiling as cod; it takes about the same time to boil.

A piece of halibut which weighs four pounds is a large dinner for a family of six or seven. It should boil forty minutes. No fish put in till the water boils. Melted butter for sauce.

Clams should boil about fifteen minutes in their own water; no other need be added, except a spoonful to keep the bottom shells from burning. It is easy to tell when they are done, by the shells starting wide open. After they are done, they should be taken from the shells, washed thoroughly in their own water, and put in a stewing pan. The water should then be strained through a cloth, so as to get out all the grit; the clams should be simmered in it ten or fifteen minutes; a little thickening of flour and water added; half a dozen slices of toasted bread or cracker; and pepper, vinegar and butter to your taste. Salt is not needed.

Four pounds of fish are enough to make a chowder for four or five people; half a dozen slices of salt pork in the bottom of the pot; hang it high, so that the pork may not burn; take it out when done very brown; put in a layer of fish, cut in lengthwise slices, then a layer formed of crackers, small or sliced onions, and potatoes sliced as thin as a four-pence, mixed with pieces of pork you have fried; then a layer of fish again, and so on. Six crackers are enough. Strew a little salt and pepper over each layer; over the whole pour a bowl-full of flour and water, enough to come up even with the surface of what you have in the pot. A sliced lemon adds to the flavor. A cup of tomato catsup is very excellent. Some people put in a cup of beer. A few clams are a pleasant addition. It should be covered so as not to let a particle of steam escape, if possible. Do not open it, except when nearly done, to taste if it be well seasoned.

Salt fish should be put in a deep plate, with just water enough to cover it, the night before you intend to cook it. It should not be boiled an instant; boiling renders it hard. It should lie in scalding hot water two or three hours. The less water is used, and the more fish is cooked at once, the better. Water thickened with flour and water while boiling, with sweet butter put in to melt, is the common sauce. It is more economical to cut salt pork into small bits, and try it till the pork is brown and crispy. It should not be done too fast, lest the sweetness be scorched out.

Salted shad and mackerel should be put into a deep plate and covered with boiling water for about ten minutes after it is thoroughly broiled, before it is buttered. This makes it tender, takes off the coat of salt, and prevents the strong oily taste, so apt to be unpleasant in preserved fish. The same rule applies to smoked salmon.

Salt fish mashed with potatoes, with good butter or pork scraps to moisten it, is nicer the second day than it was the first. The fish should be minced very fine, while it is warm. After it has got cold and dry, it is difficult to do it nicely. Salt fish needs plenty of vegetables, such as onions, beets, carrots, &c.

There is no way of preparing salt fish for breakfast, so nice as to roll it up in little balls, after it is mixed with mashed potatoes; dip it into an egg, and fry it brown.

A female lobster is not considered so good as a male. In the female, the sides of the head, or what look like cheeks, are much larger, and jut out more than those of the male. The end of a lobster is surrounded with what children call 'purses,' edged with a little fringe. If you put your hand under these to raise it, and find it springs back hard and firm, it is a sign the lobster is fresh; if they move flabbily, it is not a good omen.

Fried salt pork and apples is a favorite dish in the country; but it is seldom seen in the city. After the pork is fried, some of the fat should be taken out, lest the apples should be oily. Acid apples should be chosen, because they cook more easily; they should be cut in slices, across the whole apple, about twice or three times as thick as a new dollar. Fried till tender, and brown on both sides—laid around the pork. If you have cold potatoes, slice them and brown them in the same way.

PUDDINGS.

BAKED INDIAN PUDDING.

Indian pudding is good baked. Scald a quart of milk (skimmed milk will do,) and stir in seven table spoonfuls of sifted Indian meal, a tea-spoonful of salt, a tea-cupful of molasses, and a great spoonful of ginger, or sifted cinnamon. Baked three or four hours. If you want whey, you must be sure and pour in a little cold milk, after it is all mixed.

BOILED INDIAN PUDDING.

Indian pudding should be boiled four or five hours. Sifted Indian meal and warm milk should be stirred together pretty stiff. A little salt, and two or three great spoonfuls of molasses, added; a spoonful of ginger, if you like that spice. Boil it in a tight covered pan, or a very thick cloth; if the water gets in, it will ruin it. Leave plenty of room; for Indian swells very much. The milk with which you mix it should be merely warm; if it be scalding, the pudding will break to pieces. Some people chop sweet suet fine, and warm in the milk; others warm thin slices of sweet apple to be stirred into the pudding. Water will answer instead of milk.

FLOUR OR BATTER PUDDING.

Common flour pudding, or batter pudding, is easily made. Those who live in the country can beat up five or six eggs with a quart of milk, and a little salt, with flour enough to make it just thick enough to pour without difficulty. Those who live in the city, and are obliged to buy eggs, can do with three eggs to a quart, and more flour in proportion. Boil about three quarters of an hour.

BREAD PUDDING.

A nice pudding may be made of bits of bread. They should be crumbled and soaked in milk over night. In the morning, beat up three eggs with it, add a little salt, tie it up in a bag, or in a pan that will exclude every drop of water, and boil it little more than an hour. No puddings should be put into the pot, till the water boils. Bread prepared in the same way makes good plum-puddings. Milk enough to make it quite soft; four eggs; a little cinnamon; a spoonful of rose-water, or lemon-brandy, if you have it; a tea-cupful of molasses, or sugar to your taste, if you prefer it; a few dry, clean raisins, sprinkled in, and stirred up thoroughly, is all that is necessary. It should bake or boil two hours.

RENNET PUDDING.

If your husband brings home company when you are unprepared, rennet pudding may be made at five minutes' notice; provided you keep a piece of calf's rennet ready prepared soaking in a bottle of wine. One glass of this wine to a quart of milk will make a sort of cold custard. Sweetened with white sugar, and spiced with nutmeg, it is very good. It should be eaten immediately; in a few hours, it begins to curdle.

CUSTARD PUDDINGS.

Custard puddings sufficiently good for common use can be made with five eggs to a quart of milk, sweetened with brown sugar, and spiced with cinnamon, or nutmeg, and very little salt. It is well to boil your milk, and set it away till it gets cold. Boiling milk enriches it so much, that boiled skim-milk is about as good as new milk. A little cinnamon, or lemon peel, or peach leaves, if you do not dislike the taste, boiled in the milk, and afterwards strained from it, give a pleasant flavor. Bake fifteen or twenty minutes.

RICE PUDDINGS.

If you want a common rice pudding to retain its flavor, do not soak it, or put it in to boil when the water is cold. Wash it, tie it in a bag, leave plenty of room for it to swell, throw it in when the water boils, and let it boil about an hour and a half. The same sauce answers for all these kinds of puddings. If you have rice left cold, break it up in a little warm milk, pour custard over it, and bake it as long as you should custard. It makes very good puddings and pies.

BIRD'S NEST PUDDING.

If you wish to make what is called 'bird's nest puddings,' prepare your custard,—take eight or ten pleasant apples, pare them, and dig out the core, but leave them whole, set them in a pudding dish, pour your custard over them, and bake them about thirty minutes.

APPLE PUDDING.

A plain, unexpensive apple pudding may be made by rolling out a bit of common pie-crust, and filling it full of quartered apples; tied up in a bag, and boiled an hour and a half; if the apples are sweet, it will take two hours; for acid things cook easily. Some people like little dumplings, made by rolling up one apple, pared and cored, in a piece of crust, and tying them up in spots all over the bag. These do not need to be boiled more than an hour: three quarters is enough, if the apples are tender.

Take sweet, or pleasant flavored apples, pare them, and bore out the core, without cutting the apple in two Pill up the holes with washed rice, boil them in a bag, tied very tight, an hour, or hour and a half. Each apple should be tied up separately, in different corners of the pudding bag.

CHERRY PUDDING.

For cherry dumpling, make a paste about as rich as you make short-cake; roll it out, and put in a pint and a half, or a quart of cherries, according to the size of your family. Double the crust over the fruit, tie it up tight in a bag, and boil one hour and a half.

CRANBERRY PUDDING.

A pint of cranberries stirred into a quart of batter, made like a batter pudding, but very little stiffer, is very nice, eaten with sweet sauce.

WHORTLEBERRY PUDDING.

Whortleberries are good both in flour and Indian puddings. A pint of milk, with a little salt and a little molasses, stirred quite stiff with Indian meal, and a quart of berries stirred in gradually with a spoon, makes a good-sized pudding. Leave room for it to swell; and let it boil three hours.

When you put them into flour, make your pudding just like batter puddings; but considerably thicker, or the berries will sink. Two hours is plenty long enough to boil No pudding should be put in till the water boils. Leave room to swell.

PLUM PUDDING.

If you wish to make a really nice, soft, custard-like plum pudding, pound six crackers, or dried crusts of light bread, fine, and soak them over night in milk enough to cover them; put them in about three pints of milk, beat up six eggs, put in a little lemon-brandy, a whole nutmeg, and about three quarters of a pound of raisins which have been rubbed in flour. Bake it two hours, or perhaps a little short of that. It is easy to judge from the appearance whether it is done.

The surest way of making a light, rich plum pudding, is to spread slices of sweet light bread plentifully with butter; on each side of the slices spread abundantly raisins, or currants, nicely prepared; when they are all heaped up in a dish, cover them with milk, eggs, sugar and spice, well beat up, and prepared just as you do for custards. Let it bake about an hour.

One sauce answers for common use for all sorts of puddings. Flour-and-water stirred into boiling water, sweetened to your taste with either molasses or sugar, according to your ideas of economy; a great spoonful of rose-water, if you have it; butter half as big as a hen's egg. If you want to make it very nice, put in a glass of wine, and grate nutmeg on the top.

When you wish better sauce than common, take a quarter of a pound of butter and the same of sugar, mould them well together with your hand, add a little wine, if you choose. Make it into a lump, set it away to cool, and grate nutmeg over it.

HASTY PUDDING.

Boil water, a quart, three pints, or two quarts, according to the size of your family; sift your meal, stir five or six spoonfuls of it thoroughly into a bowl of water; when the water in the kettle boils, pour into it the contents of the bowl; stir it well, and let it boil up thick; put in salt to suit your own taste, then stand over the kettle, and sprinkle in meal, handful after handful, stirring it very thoroughly all the time, and letting it boil between whiles. When it is so thick that you stir it with great difficulty, it is about right. It takes about half an hour's cooking. Eat it with milk or molasses. Either Indian meal or rye meal may be used. If the system is in a restricted state, nothing can be better than *rye* hasty pudding and *West India* molasses. This diet would save many a one the horrors of dyspepsia.

CHEAP CUSTARDS.

One quart of milk, boiled; when boiling, add three table spoonfuls of ground rice, or rice that is boiled, mixed smooth and fine in cold milk, and one egg beaten; give it one boil up, and sweeten to your taste; peach leaves, or any spice you please, boiled in the milk.

COMMON PIES.

MINCE PIES.

Boil a tender, nice piece of beef—any piece that is clear from sinews and gristle; boil it till it is perfectly tender When it is cold, chop it very fine, and be very careful to get out every particle of bone and gristle. The suet is sweeter and better to boil half an hour or more in the liquor the beef has been boiled in; but few people do this. Pare, core, and chop the apples fine. If you use raisins, stone them. If you use currants, wash and dry them at the fire. Two pounds of beef, after it is chopped; three quarters of a pound of suet; one pound and a quarter of sugar; three pounds of apples; two pounds of currants, or raisins. Put in a gill of brandy; lemon-brandy is better, if you have any prepared. Make it quite moist with new cider. I should not think a quart would be too much; the more moist the better, if it does not spill out into the oven. A very little pepper. If you use corn meat, or tongue, for pies, it should be well soaked, and boiled very tender. If you use fresh beef, salt is necessary in the seasoning. One ounce of cinnamon, one ounce of cloves. Two nutmegs add to the pleasantness of the flavor; and a bit of sweet butter put upon the top of each pie, makes them rich; but these are not necessary. Baked three quarters of an hour. If your apples are rather sweet, grate in a whole lemon.

PUMPKIN AND SQUASH PIE.

For common family pumpkin pies, three eggs do very well to a quart of milk. Stew your pumpkin, and strain it through a sieve, or colander. Take out the seeds, and pare the pumpkin, or squash, before you stew it; but do not scrape the inside; the part nearest the seed is the sweetest part of the squash. Stir in the stewed pumpkin, till it is as thick as you can stir it round rapidly and easily. If you want to make your pie richer, make it thinner, and add another egg. One egg to a quart of milk makes very decent pies. Sweeten it to your taste, with molasses or sugar; some pumpkins require more sweetening than others. Two tea-spoonfuls of salt; two great spoonfuls of sifted cinnamon; one great spoonful of ginger. Ginger will answer very well alone for spice, if you use enough of it. The outside of a lemon grated in is nice. The more eggs, the better the pie; some put an egg to a gill of milk. They should bake from forty to fifty minutes, and even ten minutes longer, if very deep.

CARROT PIE.

Carrot pies are made like squash pies. The carrots should be boiled very tender, skinned and sifted. Both carrot pies and squash pies should be baked without an upper crust, in deep plates. To be baked an hour, in quite a warm oven.

CHERRY PIE.

Cherry pies should be baked in a deep plate. Take the cherries from the stalks, lay them in a plate, and sprinkle a little sugar, and cinnamon, according to the sweetness of the cherries. Baked with a top and bottom crust, three quarters of an hour.

WHORTLEBERRY PIE.

Whortleberries make a very good common pie, where there is a large family of children. Sprinkle a little sugar and sifted cloves into each pie. Baked in the same way, and as long, as cherry pies.

APPLE PIE.

When you make apple pies, stew your apples very little indeed; just strike them through, to make them tender. Some people do not stew them at all, but cut them up in very thin slices, and lay them in the crust. Pies made in this way may retain more of the spirit of the apple; but I do not think the seasoning mixes in as well. Put in sugar to your taste; it is impossible to make a precise rule, because apples vary so much in acidity. A very little salt, and a small piece of butter in each pie, makes them richer. Cloves and cinnamon are both suitable spice. Lemon-brandy and rose-water are both excellent. A wine-glass full of each is sufficient for three or four pies. If your apples lack spirit, grate in a whole lemon.

CUSTARD PIE.

It is a general rule to put eight eggs to a quart of milk, in making custard pies; but six eggs are a plenty for any common use. The milk should be boiled and cooled before it is used; and bits of stick-cinnamon and bits of lemon-peel boiled in it. Sweeten to your taste with clean sugar; a very little sprinkling of salt makes them taste better. Grate in a nutmeg. Bake in a deep plate. About 20 minutes are usually enough. If you are doubtful whether they are done, dip in the handle of a silver spoon, or the blade of a small knife; if it come out clean, the pie is done. Do not pour them into your plates till the minute you put them into the oven; it makes the crust wet and heavy. To be baked with an under crust only. Some people bake the under crust a little before the custard is poured in; this is to keep it from being clammy.

CRANBERRY PIE.

Cranberry pies need very little spice. A little nutmeg, or cinnamon, improves them. They need a great deal of sweetening. It is well to stew the sweetening with them; at least a part of it. It is easy to add, if you find them too sour for your taste. When cranberries are strained, and added to about their own weight in sugar, they make very delicious tarts. No upper crust.

RHUBARB STALKS, OR PERSIAN APPLE.

Rhubarb stalks, or the Persian apple, is the earliest in gradient for pies, which the spring offers. The skin should be carefully stripped, and the stalks cut into small bits, and stewed very tender. These are dear pies, for they take an enormous quantity of sugar. Seasoned like apple pies Gooseberries, currants, &c., are stewed, sweetened and seasoned like apple pies, in proportions suited to the sweetness of the fruit; there is no way to judge but by your own taste. Always remember it is more easy to add seasoning than to diminish it.

PIE CRUST.

To make pie crust for common use, a quarter of a pound of butter is enough for a half a pound of flour. Take out about a quarter part of the flour you intend to use, and lay it aside. Into the remainder of the flour rub butter thoroughly with your hands, until it is so short that a handful of it, clasped tight, will remain in a ball, without any tendency to fall in pieces. Then wet it with cold water, roll it out on a board, rub over the surface with flour, stick little lumps of butter all over it, sprinkle some flour over the butter, and roll the dough all up; flour the paste, and flour the rolling-pin; roll it lightly and quickly; flour it again; stick in bits of butter; do it up; flour the rolling-pin, and roll it quickly and lightly; and so on, till you have used up your butter. Always roll from you. Pie crust should be made as cold as possible, and set in a cool place; but be careful it does not freeze. Do not use more flour than you can help in sprinkling and rolling. The paste should not be rolled out more than three times; if rolled too much, it will not be flaky.

COMMON CAKES.

In all cakes where butter or eggs are used, the butter should be very faithfully rubbed into the flour, and the eggs beat to a foam, before the ingredients are mixed.

GINGERBREAD.

A very good way to make molasses gingerbread is to rub four pounds and a half of flour with half a pound of lard and half a pound of butter; a pint of molasses, a gill of milk, tea-cup of ginger, a tea-spoonful of dissolved pearlash stirred together. All mixed, baked in shallow pans twenty or thirty minutes.

Hard gingerbread is good to have in the family, it keeps so well. One pound of flour, half a pound of butter and sugar, rubbed into it; half a pound of sugar; great spoonful of ginger, or more, according to the strength of the ginger; a spoonful of rose-water, and a handful of caraway seed. Well beat up. Kneaded stiff enough to roll out and bake on flat pans. Bake twenty or thirty minutes.

A cake of common gingerbread can be stirred up very quick in the following way. Rub in a bit of shortening as big as an egg into a pint of flour; if you use lard, add a little salt; two or three great spoonfuls of ginger; one cup of molasses, one cup and a half of cider, and a great spoonful of dissolved pearlash, put together and poured into the shortened flour while it is foaming; to be put in the oven in a minute. It ought to be just thick enough to pour into the pans with difficulty; if these proportions make it too thin, use less liquid the next time you try. Bake about twenty minutes.

If by carelessness you let a piece of short-cake dough grow sour, put in a little pearlash and water, warm a little butter, according to the size of the dough, knead in a cup or two of sugar, (two cups, unless it is a very small bit,) two or three spoonfuls of ginger, and a little rose-water Knead it up thoroughly, roll it out on a flat pan, and bake it twenty minutes. Every thing mixed with pearlash should be put in the oven immediately.

CUP CAKE.

Cup cake is about as good as pound cake, and is cheaper. One cup of butter, two cups of sugar, three cups of flour, and four eggs, well beat together, and baked in pans or cups. Bake twenty minutes, and no more.

TEA CAKE.

There is a kind of tea cake still cheaper. Three cups of sugar, three eggs, one cup of butter, one cup of milk, a spoonful of dissolved pearlash, and four cups of flour, well beat up. If it is so stiff it will not stir easily, add a little more milk.

CIDER CAKE.

Cider cake is very good, to be baked in small loaves. One pound and a half of flour, half a pound of sugar, quarter of a pound of butter, half a pint of cider, one teaspoonful of pearlash; spice to your taste. Bake till it turns easily in the pans. I should think about half an hour.

ELECTION CAKE.

Old-fashioned election cake is made of four pounds of flour; three quarters of a pound of butter; four eggs; one pound of sugar; one pound of currants, or raisins if you choose; half a pint of good yeast; wet it with milk as soft as it can be and be moulded on a board. Set to rise over night in winter; in warm weather, three hours is usually enough for it to rise. A loaf, the size of common flour bread, should bake three quarters of an hour.

SPONGE CAKE.

The nicest way to make sponge cake, or diet-bread, is the weight of six eggs in sugar, the weight of four eggs in flour, a little rose-water. The whites and yolks should be beaten thoroughly and separately. The eggs and sugar should be well beaten together; but after the flour is sprinkled, it should not be stirred a moment longer than is necessary to mix it well; it should be poured into the pan, and got into the oven with all possible expedition. Twenty minutes is about long enough to bake. Not to be put in till some other articles have taken off the first few minutes of furious heat.

WEDDING CAKE.

Good common wedding cake may be made thus: Four pounds of flour, three pounds of butter, three pounds of sugar, four pounds of currants, two pounds of raisins, twenty-four eggs, half a pint of brandy, or lemon-brandy, one ounce of mace, and three nutmegs. A little molasses makes it dark colored, which is desirable. Half a pound of citron improves it; but it is not necessary. To be baked two hours and a half, or three hours. After the oven is cleared, it is well to shut the door for eight or ten minutes, to let the violence of the heat subside, before cake or bread is put in.

To make icing for your wedding cake, beat the whites of eggs to an entire froth, and to each egg add five teaspoonfuls of sifted loaf sugar, gradually; beat it a great while. Put it on when your cake is hot, or cold, as is most convenient. It will dry in a warm room, a short distance from a gentle fire, or in a warm oven.

LOAF CAKE.

Very good loaf cake is made with two pounds of flour, half a pound of sugar, quarter of a pound of butter, two eggs, a gill of sweet emptings, half an ounce of cinnamon, or cloves, a large spoonful of lemon-brandy, or rose-water; if it is not about as thin as goad white bread dough, add a little milk. A common sized loaf is made by these proportions. Bake about three quarters of an hour.

A handy way to make loaf cake is, to take about as much of your white bread dough, or sponge, as you think your pan will hold, and put it into a pan in which you have already beat up three or four eggs, six ounces of butter warmed, and half a pound of sugar, a spoonful of rose-water, little sifted cinnamon, or cloves. The materials should be well mixed and beat before the dough is put in; and then it should be all kneaded well together, about as stiff as white bread. Put in half a pound of currants, or raisins, with the butter, if you choose. It should Stand in the pan two or three hours to rise; and be baked about three quarters of an hour, if the pan is a common sized bread-pan.

If you have loaf cake slightly injured by time, or by being kept in the cellar, cut off all appearance of mould from the outside, wipe it with a clean cloth, and wet it well with strong brandy and water sweetened with sugar; then put it in your oven, and let the heat strike through it, for fifteen or twenty minutes. Unless very bad, this will restore the sweetness.

CARAWAY CAKES.

Take one pound of flour, three quarters of a pound of sugar, half a pound of butter, a glass of rose-water, four eggs, and half a tea-cup of caraway seed,—the materials well rubbed together and beat up. Drop them from a spoon on tin sheets, and bake them brown in rather a slow oven. Twenty minutes, or half an hour, is enough to bake them.

DOUGH-NUTS.

For dough-nuts, take one pint of flour, half a pint of sugar, three eggs, a piece of butter as big as an egg, and a tea-spoonful of dissolved pearlash. When you have no eggs, a gill of lively emptings will do; but in that case, they must be made over night. Cinnamon, rose-water, or lemon-brandy, if you have it. If you use part lard instead of butter, add a little salt. Not put in till the fat is very hot. The more fat they are fried in, the less they will soak fat.

PANCAKES.

Pancakes should be made of half a pint of milk, three great spoonfuls of sugar, one or two eggs, a tea-spoonful of dissolved pearlash, spiced with cinnamon, or cloves, a little salt, rose-water, or lemon-brandy, just as you happen to have it. Flour should be stirred in till the spoon moves round with difficulty. If they are thin, they are apt to soak fat. Have the fat in your skillet boiling hot, and drop them in with a spoon. Let them cook till thoroughly brown. The fat which is left is good to shorten other cakes. The more fat they are cooked in, the less they soak.

If you have no eggs, or wish to save them, use the above ingredients, and supply the place of eggs by two or three spoonfuls of lively emptings; but in this case they must be made five or six hours before they are cooked,—and in winter they should stand all night. A spoonful or more of N.E. rum makes pancakes light. Flip makes very nice pancakes. In this case, nothing is done but to sweeten your mug of beer with molasses; put in one glass of N.E. rum; heat it till it foams, by putting in a hot poker; and stir it up with flour as thick as other pancakes.

FRITTERS.

Flat-jacks, or fritters, do not differ from pancakes, only in being mixed softer. The same ingredients are used in about the same quantities; only most people prefer to have no sweetening put in them, because they generally have butter, sugar, and nutmeg, put on them, after they are done. Excepting for company, the nutmeg can be well dispensed with. They are not to be boiled in fat, like pancakes; the spider or griddle should be well greased, and the cakes poured on as large as you want them, when it is quite hot; when it gets brown on one side, to be turned over upon the other. Fritters are better to be baked quite thin. Either flour, Indian, or rye, is good.

Sour beer, with a spoonful of pearlash, is good both for pancakes and fritters.

If you have any cold rice left, it is nice to break it up fine in warm milk; put in a little salt; after you have put milk enough for the cakes you wish to make, (a half pint, Or more,) stir in flour till it is thick enough to pour for fritters. It does very well without an egg; but better with one. To be fried like other flat-jacks. Sugar and nutmeg are to be put on when they are buttered, if you like.

SHORT CAKE.

If you have sour milk, or butter-milk, it is well to make it into short cakes for tea. Rub in a very small bit of shortening, or three table-spoonfuls of cream, with the flour; put in a tea-spoonful of strong dissolved pearlash, into your sour milk, and mix your cake pretty stiff, to bake in the spider, on a few embers.

When people have to buy butter and lard, short cakes are not economical food. A half pint of flour will make a cake large enough to cover a common plate. Rub in thoroughly a bit of shortening as big as a hen's egg; put in a tea-spoonful of dissolved pearlash; wet it with cold water; knead it stiff enough to roll well, to bake on a plate, or in a spider. It should bake as quick as it can, and not burn. The first side should stand longer to the fire than the last.

INDIAN CAKE.

Indian cake, or bannock, is sweet and cheap food. One quart of sifted meal, two great spoonfuls of molasses, two tea-spoonfuls of salt, a bit of shortening half as big as a hen's egg, stirred together; make it pretty moist with scalding water, put it into a well greased pan, smooth over the surface with a spoon, and bake it brown on both sides, before a quick fire. A little stewed pumpkin, scalded with the meal, improves the cake. Bannock split and dipped in butter makes very nice toast. A richer Indian cake may be made by stirring one egg to a half pint of milk, sweetened with two great spoonfuls of molasses; a little ginger, or cinnamon; Indian stirred in till it is just about thick enough to pour. Spider or bake-kettle well greased; cake poured in, covered up, baked half an hour, or three quarters, according to the thickness of the cake. If you have sour milk, or butter-milk, it is very nice for this kind of cake; the acidity corrected by a tea-spoonful of dissolved pearlash. It is a rule never to use pearlash for Indian, unless to correct the sourness of milk; it injures the flavor of the meal.

Nice suet improves all kinds of Indian cakes very much.

Two cups of Indian meal, one table-spoonful molasses, two cups milk, a little salt, a handful flour, a little saleratus, mixed up thin, and poured into a buttered bake-kettle, hung over the fire uncovered, until you can bear your finger upon it, and then set down before the fire. Bake half an hour.

BREAD, YEAST, &C.

It is more difficult to give rules for making bread than for anything else; it depends so much on judgment and experience. In summer, bread should be mixed with cold water; during a chilly, damp spell, the water should be slightly warm; in severe cold weather, it should be mixed quite warm, and set in a warm place during the night. If your yeast is new and lively, a small quantity will make the bread rise; if it be old and heavy, it will take more. In these things I believe wisdom must be gained by a few mistakes.

Six quarts of meal will make two good sized loaves of *Brown Bread*. Some like to have it half Indian meal and half rye meal; others prefer it one third Indian, and two thirds rye. Many mix their brown bread over night; but there is no need of it; and it is more likely to sour, particularly in summer. If you do mix it the night before you bake it, you must not put in more than half the yeast I am about to mention, unless the weather is intensely cold. The meal should be sifted separately. Put the Indian in your bread-pan, sprinkle a little salt among it, and wet it thoroughly with scalding water. Stir it up while you are scalding it. Be sure and have hot water enough; for Indian absorbs a great deal of water. When it is cool, pour in your rye; add two gills of lively yeast, and mix it with water as stiff as you can knead it. Let it stand an hour and a half, in a cool place in summer, on the hearth in winter. It should be put into a very hot oven, and baked three or four hours. It is all the better for remaining in the oven over night.

Flour Bread should have a sponge set the night before. The sponge should be soft enough to pour; mixed with water, warm or cold, according to the temperature of the weather. One gill of lively yeast is enough to put into sponge for two loaves. I should judge about three pints of sponge would be right for two loaves. The warmth of the place in which the sponge is set, should be determined by the coldness of the weather. If your sponge looks frothy in the morning, it is a sign your bread will be good; if it does not rise, stir in a little more emptings; if it rises too much, taste of it, to see if it has any acid taste; if so, put in a tea-spoonful of pearlash when you mould in your flour; be sure the pearlash is well dissolved in water; if there are little lumps, your bread will be full of bitter spots. About an hour before your oven is ready, stir in flour into your sponge till it is stiff enough to lay on a well floured board or table. Knead it up pretty stiff, and put it into well greased pans, and let it stand in a cool or warm place, according to the weather. If the oven is ready, put them in fifteen or twenty minutes after the dough begins to rise up and crack; if the oven is not ready, move the pans to a cooler spot, to prevent the dough from becoming sour by too much rising. Common sized loaves will bake in three quarters of an hour. If they slip easily in the pans, it is a sign they are done. Some people do not set a soft sponge for flour bread; they knead it up all ready to put in the pans the night before, and leave it to rise. White bread and pies should not be set in the oven until the brown bread and beans have been in half an hour. If the oven be too hot, it will bind the crust so suddenly that the bread cannot rise; if it be too cold, the bread will fall. Flour bread should not be too stiff.

Some people like one third Indian in their flour. Others like one third rye; and some think the nicest of all bread is one third Indian, one third rye, and one third flour, made according to the directions for flour bread. When Indian is used, it should be salted, and scalded, before the other meal is put in. A mixture of other grains is economical when flour is high.

Dyspepsia Bread.—The American Farmer publishes the following receipt for making bread, which has proved highly salutary to persons afflicted with that complaint, viz:—Three quarts unbolted wheat meal; one quart soft water, warm, but not hot; one gill of fresh yeast; one gill of molasses, or not, as may suit the taste; one tea-spoonful of saleratus.

This will make two loaves, and should remain in the oven at least one hour; and when taken out, placed where they will cool gradually. Dyspepsia crackers can be made with unbolted flour, water and saleratus.

To make Rice Bread.—Boil a pint of rice soft; add a pint of leaven; then, three quarts of the flour; put it to rise in a tin or earthen vessel until it has risen sufficiently; divide it into three parts; then bake it as other bread, and you will have three large loaves.

Heating ovens must be regulated by experience and observation. There is a difference in wood in giving out heat; there is a great difference in the construction of ovens; and when an oven is extremely cold, either on account of the weather, or want of use, it must be heated more. Economical people heat ovens with pine wood, fagots, brush, and such light stuff. If you have none but hard wood, you must remember that it makes very hot coals, and therefore less of it will answer. A smart fire for an hour and a half is a general rule for common sized family ovens, provided brown bread and beans are to be baked. An hour is long enough to heat an oven for flour bread. Pies bear about as much heat as flour bread: pumpkin pies will bear more. If you are afraid your oven is too hot, throw in a little flour, and shut it up for a minute. If it scorches black immediately, the heat is too furious; if it merely browns, it is right. Some people wet an old broom two or three times, and turn it round near the top of die oven till it dries; this prevents pies and cake from scorching on the top. When you go into a new house, heat your oven two or three times, to get it seasoned, before you use it. After the wood is burned, rake the coals over the bottom of the oven, and let them lie a few minutes.

Those who make their own bread should make yeast too. When bread is nearly out, always think whether yeast is in readiness; for it takes a day and night to prepare it. One handful of hops, with two or three handsful of malt and rye bran, should be boiled fifteen or twenty minutes, in two quarts of water, then strained, hung on to boil again, and thickened with half a pint of rye and water stirred up quite thick, and a little molasses; boil it a minute or two, and then take it off to cool. When just about lukewarm, put in a cupful of good lively yeast, and set it in a cool place in summer, and warm place in winter. If it is too warm when you put in the old yeast, all the spirit will be killed.

In summer, yeast sours easily; therefore make but little at a time. Bottle it when it gets well a working; it keeps better when the air is corked out. If you find it acid, but still spirited, put a little pearlash to it, as you use it; but by no means put it into your bread unless it foams up bright and lively as soon as the pearlash mixes with it. Never keep yeast in tin; it destroys its life.

There is another method of making yeast, which is much easier, and I think quite as good. Stir rye and cold water, till you make a stiff thickening. Then pour in boiling water, and stir it all the time, till you make it as thin as the yeast you buy; three or four table spoons heaping full are enough for a quart of water. When it gets about cold, put in half a pint of lively yeast. When it works well, bottle it; but if very lively, do not cork your bottle *very* tight, for fear it will burst. Always think to make new yeast before the old is gone; so that you may have some to work with. Always wash and scald your bottle clean after it has contained sour yeast. Beware of freezing yeast.

Milk yeast is made quicker than any other. A pint of new milk with a tea-spoonful of salt, and a large spoon of flour stirred in, set by the fire to keep lukewarm, will make yeast fit for use in an hour. Twice the quantity of common yeast is necessary, and unless used soon is good for nothing. Bread made of this yeast dries sooner. It is convenient in summer, when one wants to make biscuits suddenly.

A species of leaven may be made that will keep any length of time. Three ounces of hops in a pail of water boiled down to a quart; strain it, and stir in a quart of rye meal while boiling hot. Cool it, and add half a pint of good yeast; after it has risen a few hours, thicken it with Indian meal stiff enough to roll out upon a board; then put it in the sun and air a few days to dry. A piece of this cake two inches square, dissolved in warm water, and thickened with a little flour, will make a large loaf of bread.

Potatoes make very good yeast. Mash three large potatoes fine; pour a pint of boiling water over them; when almost cold, stir in two spoonfuls of flour, two of molasses, and a cup of good yeast. This yeast should be used while new.

PRESERVES, &C.

Economical people will seldom use preserves, except for sickness. They are unhealthy, expensive, and useless to those who are well. Barberries preserved in molasses are very good for common use. Boil the molasses, skim it, throw in the barberries, and simmer them till they are soft. If you wish to lay by a few for sickness, preserve them in sugar by the same rule as other preserves. Melt the sugar, skim it, throw in the barberries; when done soft, take them out, and throw in others.

A pound of sugar to a pound of fruit is the rule for all preserves. The sugar should be melted over a fire moderate enough not to scorch it. When melted, it should be skimmed clean, and the fruit dropped in to simmer till it is soft. Plums, and things of which the skin is liable to be broken, do better to be put in little jars, with their weight of sugar, and the jars set in a kettle of boiling water, till the fruit is done. See the water is not so high as to boil into the jars.

When you put preserves in jars, lay a white paper, thoroughly wet with brandy, flat upon the surface of the preserves, and cover them carefully from the air. If they begin to mould, scald them by setting them in the oven till boiling hot. Glass is much better than earthen for preserves; they are not half as apt to ferment.

CURRANT JELLY.

Currant jelly is a useful thing for sickness. If it be necessary to wash your currants, be sure they are thoroughly drained, or your jelly will be thin. Break them up with a pestle, and squeeze them through a cloth. Put a pint of clean sugar to a pint of juice, and boil it slowly, till it becomes ropy. Great care must be taken not to do it too fast; it is spoiled by being scorched. It should be frequently skimmed while simmering. If currants are put in a jar, and kept in boiling water, and cooked before they are strained, they are more likely to keep a long time without fermenting.

CURRANT WINE.

Those who have more currants than they have money, will do well to use no wine but of their own manufacture. Break and squeeze the currants, put three pounds and a half of sugar to two quarts of juice and two quarts of water. Put in a keg or barrel. Do not close the bung tight for three or four days, that the air may escape while it is fermenting. After it is done fermenting, close it up tight. Where raspberries are plenty, it is a great improvement to use half raspberry juice, and half currant juice. Brandy is unnecessary when the above-mentioned proportions are observed. It should not be used under a year or two. Age improves it.

RASPBERRY SHRUB.

Raspberry shrub mixed with water is a pure, delicious drink for summer; and in a country where raspberries are abundant, it is good economy to make it answer instead of Port and Catalonia wine. Put raspberries in a pan, and scarcely cover them with strong vinegar. Add a pint of sugar to a pint of juice; (of this you can judge by first trying your pan to see how much it holds;) scald it, skim it, and bottle it when cold.

COFFEE.

As substitutes for coffee, some use dry brown bread crusts, and roast them; others soak rye grain in rum, and roast it; others roast peas in the same way as coffee. None of these are very good; and peas so used are considered unhealthy. Where there is a large family of apprentices and workmen, and coffee is very dear, it may be worth while to use the substitutes, or to mix them half and half with coffee; but, after all, the best economy is to go without.

French coffee is so celebrated, that it may be worth while to tell how it is made; though no prudent housekeeper will make it, unless she has boarders, who are willing to pay for expensive cooking.

The coffee should be roasted more than is common with us; it should not hang drying over the fire, but should be roasted quick; it should be ground soon after roasting, and used as soon as it is ground. Those who pride themselves on first-rate coffee, burn it and grind it every morning. The powder should be placed in the coffee-pot in the proportions of an ounce to less than a pint of water. The water should be poured upon the coffee boiling hot. The coffee should be kept at the boiling point; but should not boil. Coffee made in this way must be made in a biggin. It would not be clear in a common coffee-pot.

A bit of fish-skin as big as a ninepence, thrown into coffee while it is boiling, tends to make it clear. If you use it just as it comes from the salt-fish, it will be apt to give an unpleasant taste to the coffee: it should be washed clean as a bit of cloth, and hung up till perfectly dry. The white of eggs, and even egg shells are good to settle coffee. Rind of salt pork is excellent.

Some people think coffee is richer and clearer for having a bit of sweet butter, or a whole egg, dropped in and stirred, just before it is done roasting, and ground up, shell and all, with the coffee. But these things are not economical, except on a farm, where butter and eggs are plenty. A half a gill of cold water, poured in after you take your coffee-pot off the fire, will *usually* settle the coffee.

If you have not cream for coffee, it is a very great improvement to boil your milk, and use it while hot.

CHOCOLATE.

Many people boil chocolate in a coffee-pot; but I think it is better to boil it in a skillet, or something open. A piece of chocolate about as big as a dollar is the usual quantity for a quart of water; but some put in more, and some less. When it boils, pour in as much milk as you like and let them boil together three or four minutes. It is much richer with the milk boiled in it. Put the sugar in either before or after, as you please. Nutmeg improves it. The chocolate should be scraped fine before it is put into the water.

TEA.

Young Hyson is supposed to be a more profitable tea than Hyson; but though the *quantity* to a pound is greater, it has not so much *strength*. In point of economy, therefore, there is not much difference between them. Hyson tea and Souchong mixed together, half and half, is a pleasant beverage, and is more healthy than green tea alone. Be sure that water boils before it is poured upon tea. A tea-spoonful to each person, and one extra thrown in, is a good rule. Steep ten or fifteen minutes.

PICKLES.

Musk-melons should be picked for mangoes, when they are green and hard. They should be cut open after they have been in salt water ten days, the inside scraped out clean, and filled with mustard-seed, allspice, horseradish, small onions, &c., and sewed up again. Scalding vinegar poured upon them.

When walnuts are so ripe that a pin will go into them easily, they are ready for pickling. They should be soaked twelve days in very strong cold salt and water, which has been boiled and skimmed. A quantity of vinegar, enough to cover them well, should be boiled with whole pepper, mustard-seed, small onions, or garlic, cloves, ginger, and horseradish; this should not be poured upon them till it is cold. They should be pickled a few months before they are eaten. To be kept close covered; for the air softens them. The liquor is an excellent catsup to be eaten on fish.

Put peppers into strong salt and water, until they become yellow; then turn them green by keeping them in warm salt and water, shifting them every two days. Then drain them, and pour scalding vinegar over them. A bag of mustard-seed is an improvement. If there is mother in vinegar, scald and strain it.

Cucumbers should be in weak brine three or four days after they are picked; then they should be put in a tin or wooden pail of clean water, and kept slightly warm in the kitchen corner for two or three days. Then take as much vinegar as you think your pickle jar will hold; scald it with pepper, allspice, mustard-seed, flag-root, horseradish, &c., if you happen to have them; half of them will spice the pickles very well. Throw in a bit of alum as big as a walnut; this serves to make pickles hard. Skim the vinegar clean, and pour it scalding hot upon the cucumbers. Brass vessels are not healthy for preparing anything acid. Red cabbages need no other pickling than scalding, spiced vinegar poured upon them, and suffered to remain eight or ten days before you eat them. Some people think it improves them to keep them in salt and water twenty-four hours before they are pickled.

If you find your pickles soft and insipid, it is owing to the weakness of the vinegar. Throw away the vinegar, (or keep it to clean your brass kettles,) then cover your pickles with strong, scalding vinegar, into which a little allspice, ginger, horseradish and alum have been thrown. By no means omit a pretty large bit of alum. Pickles attended to in this way, will keep for years, and be better and better every year.

Some people prefer pickled nasturtion-seed to capers. They should be kept several days after they are gathered, and then covered with boiling vinegar, and bottled when cold. They are not fit to be eaten for some months.

Martinoes are prepared in nearly the same way as other pickles. The salt and water in which they are put, two or three days previous to pickling, should be changed every day; because martinoes are very apt to become soft. No spice should be used but allspice, cloves, and cinnamon. The martinoes and the spice should be scalded *in* the vinegar, instead of pouring the vinegar *over* the martinoes.

BEER.

Beer is a good family drink. A handful of hops, to a pailful of water, and a half-pint of molasses, makes good hop beer. Spruce mixed with hops is pleasanter than hops alone. Boxberry, fever-bush, sweet fern, and horseradish make a good and healthy diet-drink. The winter evergreen, or rheumatism weed, thrown in, is very beneficial to humors. Be careful and not mistake kill-lamb for winter-evergreen; they resemble each other. Malt mixed with a few hops makes a weak kind of beer; but it is cool and pleasant; it needs less molasses than hops alone. The rule is about the same for all beer. Boil the ingredients two or three hours, pour in a half-pint of molasses to a pailful, while the beer is scalding hot. Strain the beer, and when about lukewarm, put a pint of lively yeast to a barrel. Leave the bung loose till the beer is done working; you can ascertain this by observing when the froth subsides. If your family be large, and the beer will be drank rapidly, it may as well remain in the barrel; but if your family be small, fill what bottles you have with it;

it keeps better bottled. A raw potato or two, cut up and thrown in, while the ingredients are boiling, is said to make beer spirited.

Ginger beer is made in the following proportions:— One cup of ginger, one pint of molasses, one pail and a half of water, and a cup of lively yeast. Most people scald the ginger in half a pail of water, and then fill it up with a pailful of cold; but in very hot weather some people stir it up cold. Yeast must not be put in till it is cold, or nearly cold. If not to be drank within twenty-four hours, it must be bottled as soon as it works.

Table beer should be drawn off into *stone* jugs, with a lump of white sugar in each, securely corked. It is brisk and pleasant, and continues good several months.

Potato cheese is much sought after in various parts of Europe. I do not know whether it is worth seeking after, or not. The following is the receipt for making:—Select good white potatoes, boil them, and, when cold, peel and reduce them to a pulp with a rasp or mortar; to five pounds of this pulp, which must be very uniform and homogeneous, add a pint of sour milk and the requisite portion of salt; knead the whole well, cover it, and let it remain three or four days, according to the season; then knead it afresh, and place the cheeses in small baskets, when they will part with their superfluous moisture; dry them in the shade, and place them in layers in large pots or kegs, where they may remain a fortnight. The older they are, the finer they become.

This cheese has the advantage of never engendering worms, and of being preserved fresh for many years, provided it is kept in a dry place, and in well closed vessels.

GENERAL MAXIMS FOR HEALTH.

Rise early. Eat simple food. Take plenty of exercise. Never fear a little fatigue. Let not children be dressed in tight clothes; it is necessary their limbs and muscles should have full play, if you wish for either health or beauty.

Avoid the necessity of a physician, if you can, by careful attention to your diet. Eat what best agrees with your system, and resolutely abstain from what hurts you, however well you may like it. A few days' abstinence, and cold water for a beverage, has driven off many an approaching disease.

If you find yourself really ill, send for a good physician. Have nothing to do with quacks; and do not tamper with quack medicines. You do not know what they are; and what security have you that they know what they are?

Wear shoes that are large enough. It not only produces corns, but makes the feet misshapen, to cramp them.

Wash very often, and rub the skin thoroughly with a hard brush.

Let those who love to be invalids drink strong green tea, eat pickles, preserves, and rich pastry. As far as possible, eat and sleep at regular hours.

Wash the eyes thoroughly in cold water every morning. Do not read or sew at twilight, or by too dazzling a light. If far-sighted, read with rather less light, and with the book somewhat nearer to the eye, than you desire. If nearsighted, read with a book as far off as possible. Both these imperfections may be diminished in this way.

Clean teeth in pure water two or three times a day; but, above all, be sure to have them clean before you go to bed.

Have your bed-chamber well aired; and have fresh bed linen every week. Never have the wind blowing directly upon you from open windows during the night. It is *not* healthy to sleep in heated rooms.

Let children have their bread and milk before they have been long up. Cold water and a run in the fresh air before breakfast.

Too frequent use of an ivory comb injures the hair. Thorough combing, washing in suds, or N.E. rum, and thorough brushing, will keep it in order; and the washing does not injure the hair, as is generally supposed. Keep children's hair cut close until ten or twelve years old; it is better for health and the beauty of the hair. Do not sleep with hair frizzled, or braided. Do not make children cross-eyed, by having hair hang about their foreheads, where they see it continually.

HINTS TO PERSONS
OF MODERATE FORTUNE

[FIRST PUBLISHED IN THE MASSACHUSETTS JOURNAL.]

When clouds are seen, wise men put on their cloaks.—
SHAKSPEARE.

FURNITURE.

The prevailing evil of the present day is extravagance. I know very well that the old are too prone to preach about modern degeneracy, whether they have cause or not; but, laugh as we may at the sage advice of our fathers, it is too plain that our present expensive habits are productive of much domestic unhappiness, and injurious to public prosperity. Our wealthy people copy all the foolish and extravagant caprice of European fashion, without considering that we have not their laws of inheritance among us; and that our frequent changes of policy render property far more precarious here than in the old world. However, it is not to the rich I would speak. They have an undoubted right to spend their thousands as they please; and if they spend them ridiculously, it is consoling to reflect that they must, in some way or other, benefit the poorer classes. People of moderate fortunes have likewise an unquestioned right to dispose of their hundreds as they please; but I would ask, Is it *wise* to risk your happiness in a foolish attempt to keep up with the opulent? Of what *use* is the effort which takes so much of your time, and *all* of your income? Nay, if any unexpected change in affairs should deprive you of a few yearly hundreds, you will find your expenses have *exceeded* your income; thus the foundation of an accumulating debt will be laid, and your family will have formed habits but poorly calculated to save you from the threatened ruin. Not one valuable friend will be gained by living beyond your means, and old age will be left to comparative, if not to utter poverty.

There is nothing in which the extravagance of the present day strikes me so forcibly as the manner in which our young people of moderate fortune furnish their houses.

A few weeks since, I called upon a farmer's daughter, who had lately married a young physician of moderate talents, and destitute of fortune. Her father had given her, at her marriage, all he ever expected to give her: viz. two thousand dollars. Yet the lower part of her house was furnished with as much splendor as we usually find among the wealthiest. The whole two thousand had been expended upon Brussels

143

carpets, alabaster vases, mahogany chairs, and marble tables. I afterwards learned that the more useful household utensils had been forgotten; and that, a few weeks after her wedding, she was actually obliged to apply to her husband for money to purchase baskets, iron spoons, clothes-lines, &c.; and her husband, made irritable by the want of money, pettishly demanded why she had bought so many things they did not want. Did the doctor gain any patients, or she a single friend, by offering their visiters water in richly-cut glass tumblers, or serving them with costly damask napkins, instead of plain soft towels? No; their foolish vanity made them less happy, and no more respectable.

Had the young lady been content with Kidderminster carpets, and tasteful vases of her own making, she might have put *one* thousand dollars at interest; and had she obtained six per cent., it would have clothed her as well as the wife of any man, who depends merely upon his own industry, ought to be clothed. This would have saved much domestic disquiet; for, after all, human nature is human nature; and a wife is never better beloved, because she teases for money.

EDUCATION OF DAUGHTERS.

There is no subject so much connected with individual happiness and national prosperity as the education of daughters. It is a true, and therefore an old remark, that the situation and prospects of a country may be justly estimated by the character of its women; and we all know how hard it is to engraft upon a woman's character habits and principles to which she was unaccustomed in her girlish days. It is always extremely difficult, and sometimes utterly impossible. Is the present education of young ladies likely to contribute to their own ultimate happiness, or to the welfare of the country? There are many honorable exceptions; but we do think the general tone of female education is bad. The greatest and most universal error is, teaching girls to exaggerate the importance of getting married; and of course to place an undue importance upon the polite attentions of gentlemen. It was but a few days since, I heard a pretty and sensible girl say, 'Did you ever see a man so ridiculously fond of his daughters as Mr. ——? He is all the time with them. The other night, at the party, I went and took Anna away by mere force; for I knew she must feel dreadfully to have her father waiting upon her all the time, while the other girls were talking with the beaux.' And another young friend of mine said, with an air most laughably serious, 'I don't think Harriet and Julia enjoyed themselves at all last night. Don't you think, nobody but their *brother* offered to hand them to the supper-room?'

That a mother should wish to see her daughters happily married, is natural and proper; that a young lady should be pleased with polite attentions is likewise natural and innocent;

but this undue anxiety, this foolish excitement about showing off the attentions of somebody, no matter whom, is attended with consequences seriously injurious. It promotes envy and rivalship; it leads our young girls to spend their time between the public streets, the ball room, and the toilet; and, worst of all, it leads them to contract engagements, without any knowledge of their own hearts, merely for the sake of being married as soon as their companions. When married, they find themselves ignorant of the important duties of domestic life; and its quiet pleasures soon grow tiresome to minds worn out by frivolous excitements. If they remain unmarried, their disappointment and discontent are, of course, in proportion to their exaggerated idea of the eclat attendant upon having a lover. The evil increases in a startling ratio; for these girls, so injudiciously educated, will, nine times out of ten, make injudicious mothers, aunts, and friends; thus follies will be accumulated unto the third and fourth generation. Young ladies should be taught that usefulness is happiness, and that all other things are but incidental. With regard to matrimonial speculations, they should be taught nothing! Leave the affections to nature and to truth, and all will end well. How many can I at this moment recollect, who have made themselves unhappy by marrying for the sake of the *name* of being married! How many do I know, who have been instructed to such watchfulness in the game, that they have lost it by trumping their own tricks!

One great cause of the vanity, extravagance and idleness that are so fast growing upon our young ladies, is the absence of *domestic education.* By domestic education, I do not mean the sending daughters into the kitchen some half dozen times, to weary the patience of the cook, and to boast of it the next day in the parlor. I mean two or three years spent with a mother, assisting her in her duties, instructing brothers and sisters, and taking care of their own clothes. This is the way to make them happy, as well as good wives; for, being early accustomed to the duties of life, they will sit lightly as well as gracefully upon them.

But what time do modern girls have for the formation of quiet, domestic habits? Until sixteen they go to school; sometimes these years are judiciously spent, and sometimes they are half wasted; too often they are spent in acquiring the *elements* of a thousand sciences, without being thoroughly acquainted with any; or in a variety of accomplishments of very doubtful value to people of moderate fortune. As soon as they leave school, (and sometimes before,) they begin a round of balls and parties, and staying with gay young friends. Dress and flattery take up all their thoughts. What time have they to learn to be useful? What time have they to cultivate the still and gentle affections, which must, in every situation of life, have such an important effect on a woman's character and happiness?

As far as parents can judge what will be a daughter's station, education should be adapted to it; but it is well to remember that it is always easy to know how to spend riches, and always safe to know how to bear poverty.

A superficial acquaintance with such accomplishments as music and drawing is useless and undesirable. They should not be attempted unless there is taste, talent, and time enough to attain excellence. I have frequently heard young women of moderate fortune say, 'I have not opened my piano these five years. I wish I had the money expended upon it. If I had employed as much time in learning useful things, I should have been better fitted for the cares of my family.'

By these remarks I do not mean to discourage an attention to the graces of life. Gentility and taste are always lovely in all situations. But good things, carried to excess, are often productive of bad consequences. When accomplishments and dress interfere with the duties and permanent happiness of life, they are unjustifiable and displeasing; but where there is a solid foundation in mind and heart, all those elegancies are but becoming ornaments.

Some are likely to have more use for them than others; and they are justified in spending more time and money upon them. But no one should be taught to consider them valuable for mere parade and attraction. Making the education of girl, about sixteen, practising on the piano, while an elderly lady beside her was darning her stockings. I was told (for the mother was proud of bringing up her child so genteelly) that the daughter had almost forgotten how to sew, and that a woman was hired into the house to do her mending! 'But why,' said I, 'have you suffered your daughter to be ignorant of so useful an employment? If she is poor, the knowledge will be necessary to her; if she is rich, it is the easiest thing in the world to lay it aside, if she chooses; she will merely be a better judge whether her work is well done by others.' 'That is true,' replied the mother; 'and I always meant she should learn; but she never has seemed to have any time. When she was eight years old, she could put a shirt together pretty well; but since that, her music, and her dancing, and her school, have taken up her whole time. I did mean she should learn some domestic habits this winter; but she has so many visiters, and is obliged to go out so much, that I suppose I must give it up. I don't like to say too much about it; for, poor girl! she does so love company, and she does so hate anything like care and confinement! *Now* is her time to enjoy herself, you know. Let her take all the comfort she can, while she is single!' 'But,' said I, 'you wish her to marry some time or other; and, in all probability, she will marry. When will she learn how to perform the duties, which are necessary and important to every mistress of a family?' 'Oh, she will learn them when she is obliged to,' answered the injudicious mother; 'at all events, I am determined she shall enjoy herself while she is young.'

And this is the way I have often heard mothers talk! Yet, could parents foresee the almost inevitable consequences of such a system, I believe the weakest and vainest would abandon the false and dangerous theory. What a lesson is taught a girl in that sentence, '*Let her enjoy herself all she can, while she is single.*' Instead of representing domestic life as the gathering place of the deepest and purest affections; as the sphere of woman's *enjoyments* as well as of her *duties*; as, indeed, the whole world to her; that one pernicious sentence teaches a girl to consider matrimony desirable because 'a good match' is a triumph of vanity, and it is deemed respectable to be 'well settled in the world;' but that it is a necessary sacrifice of her freedom and her gayety. And then how many affectionate dispositions have been trained into heartlessness, by being taught that the indulgence of indolence and vanity were necessary to their happiness; and that to have this indulgence, they *must* marry money! But who that marries for money, in this land of precarious fortunes, can tell how soon they will lose the glittering temptation, to which they have been willing to sacrifice so much? And even if riches last as long as life, the evil is not remedied. Education has given a wrong end and aim to their whole existence; they have been taught to look for happiness where it never can be found, viz. in the absence of all occupation, or the unsatisfactory and ruinous excitement of fashionable competition.

The difficulty is, education does not usually point the female heart to its only true resting-place. That dear English word '*home*,' is not half so powerful a talisman as '*the world*.' Instead of the salutary truth, that happiness is *in* duty, they are taught to consider the two things totally distinct; and that whoever seeks one, must sacrifice the other.

The fact is, our girls have no *home education*. When quite young, they are sent to schools where no feminine employments, no domestic habits, can be learned; and there they continue till they 'come out' into the world. After this, few find any time to arrange, and make use of, the mass of elementary knowledge they have acquired; and fewer still have either leisure or taste for the inelegant, every-day duties of life. Thus prepared, they enter upon matrimony. Those early habits, which would have made domestic care a light and easy task, have never been taught, for fear it would interrupt their happiness; and the result is, that when cares come, as come they must, they find them misery. I am convinced that indifference and dislike between husband and wife are more frequently occasioned by this great error in education, than by any other cause.

The bride is awakened from her delightful dream, in which carpets, vases, sofas, white gloves, and pearl earrings, are oddly jumbled up with her lover's looks and promises.

Perhaps she would be surprised if she knew exactly how *much* of the fascination of being engaged was owing to the aforesaid inanimate concern. Be that as it will, she is awakened by the unpleasant conviction that cares devolve upon her. And what effect does this produce upon her character? Do the holy and tender influences of domestic love render self-denial and exertion a bliss? No! They would have done so, had she been *properly educated*; but now she gives way to unavailing fretfulness and repining; and her husband is at first pained, and finally disgusted, by hearing, 'I never knew what care was when I lived in my father's house.' 'If I were to live my life over again, I would remain single as long as I could, without the risk of being an old maid.' How injudicious, how short-sighted is the policy, which thus mars the whole happiness of life, in order to make a few brief years more gay and brilliant! I have known many instances of domestic ruin and discord produced by this mistaken indulgence of mothers. *I never knew but one, where the victim had moral courage enough to change all her early habits.* She was a young, pretty, and very amiable girl; but brought up to be perfectly useless; a rag baby would, to all intents and purposes, have been as efficient a partner. She married a young lawyer, without property, but with good and increasing practice. She meant to be a good wife, but she did not know how. Her wastefulness involved him in debt. He did not reproach, though he tried to convince and instruct rigid economy and patient toil. Yet I would not that servile and laborious employment should be forced upon the young. I would merely have each one educated according to his probable situation in life; and be taught that whatever is his duty, is honorable; and that no merely external circumstance can in reality injure true dignity of character. I would not cramp a boy's energies by compelling him always to cut wood, or draw water; but I would teach him not to be ashamed, should his companions happen to find him doing either one or the other. A few days since, I asked a grocer's lad to bring home some articles I had just purchased at his master's. The bundle was large; he was visibly reluctant to take it; and wished very much that I should send for it. This, however, was impossible; and he subdued his pride; but when I asked him to take back an empty bottle which belonged to the store, he, with a mortified look, begged me to do it up neatly in a paper, that it might look like a small package. Is this boy likely to be happier for cherishing a foolish pride, which will forever be jarring against his duties? Is he in reality one whit more respectable than the industrious lad who sweeps stores, or carries bottles, without troubling himself with the idea that all the world is observing his little unimportant self? For, in relation to the rest of the world, each individual is unimportant; and he alone is wise who forms his habits according to his own wants, his own prospects, and his own principles.

TRAVELLING AND PUBLIC AMUSEMENTS.

There is one kind of extravagance rapidly increasing in this country, which, in its effects on our purses and our *habits*, is one of the worst kinds of extravagance; I mean the rage for travelling, and for public amusements. The good old home habits of our ancestors are breaking up—it will be well if our virtue and our freedom do not follow them! It is easy to laugh at such prognostics,—and we are well aware that the virtue we preach is considered almost obsolete,—but let any reflecting mind inquire how decay has begun in all republics, and then let them calmly ask themselves whether we are in no danger, in departing thus rapidly from the simplicity and industry of our forefathers.

Nations do not plunge *at once* into ruin—governments do not change *suddenly*—the causes which bring about the final blow, are scarcely perceptible in the beginning; but they increase in numbers, and in power; they press harder and harder upon the energies and virtue of a people; and the last steps only are alarmingly hurried and irregular. A republic without industry, economy, and integrity, is Samson shorn of his locks. A luxurious and idle *republic*! Look at the phrase!—The words were never made to be married together; every body sees it would be death to one of them.

And are not *we* becoming luxurious and idle? Look at our steamboats, and stages, and taverns! There you will find mechanics, who have left debts and employment to take care of themselves, while they go to take a peep at the great canal, or the opera-dancers. There you will find domestics all agog for their wages-worth of travelling; why should they look out for 'a rainy day?' There are hospitals enough to provide for them in sickness; and as for marrying, they have no idea of that, till they can find a man who will support them genteelly. There you will find mothers, who have left the children at home with Betsey, while they go to improve their minds at the Mountain House, or the Springs.

If only the rich did this, all would be well. They benefit others, and do not injure themselves. In any situation, idleness is their curse, and uneasiness is the tax they must pay for affluence; but their restlessness is as great a benefit to the community as the motions of Prince Esterhazy, when at every step the pearls drop from his coat.

People of moderate fortune have just as good a right to travel as the wealthy; but is it not unwise? Do they not injure themselves and their families? You say travelling is cheap. So is staying at home. Besides, do you count *all* the costs?

The money you pay for stages and steamboats is the smallest of the items. There are clothes bought which would not otherwise be bought; those clothes are worn out and defaced twenty times as quick as they would have been at home; children are perhaps left with domestics, or strangers; their health and morals, to say the least, under very uncertain influence; your substance is wasted in your absence by those who have no self-interest to prompt them to carefulness; you form an acquaintance with a multitude of people, who will be sure to take your house in their way, when they travel next year; and finally, you become so accustomed to excitement, that home appears insipid, and it requires no small effort to return to the quiet routine of your duties. And what do you get in return for all this? Some pleasant scenes, which will soon seem to you like a dream; some pleasant faces, which you will never see again; and much of crowd, and toil, and dust, and bustle.

I once knew a family which formed a striking illustration of my remarks. The man was a farmer, and his wife was an active, capable woman, with more of ambition than sound policy. Being in debt, they resolved to take fashionable boarders from Boston, during the summer season. These boarders, at the time of their arrival, were projecting a jaunt to the Springs; and they talked of Lake George crystals, and Canadian music, and English officers, and 'dark blue Ontario,' with its beautiful little brood of *lakelets*, as Wordsworth would call them; and how one lady was dressed superbly at Saratoga; and how another was scandalized for always happening to drop her fan in the vicinity of the wealthiest beaux. All this fired the quiet imagination of the good farmer's wife; and no sooner had the boarders departed to enjoy themselves in spite of heat, and dust, and fever-

and-ague, than she stated her determination to follow them. 'Why have we not as good a right to travel, as they have?' said she; 'they have paid us money enough to go to Niagara with; and it really is a shame for people to live and die so ignorant of their own country.' 'But then we want the money to pay for that stock, which turned out unlucky, you know.' 'Oh, that can be done next summer; we can always get boarders enough, and those that will pay handsomely. Give the man a mortgage of the house, to keep him quiet till next summer.' 'But what will you do with the children?' 'Sally is a very smart girl; I am sure she will take as good care of them as if I were at home.'

To make a long story short, the farmer and his wife concluded to go to Quebec, just to show they had a *right* to put themselves to inconvenience, if they pleased. They went; spent all their money; had a watch stolen from them in the steamboat; were dreadfully sea-sick off Point Judith; came home tired, and dusty; found the babe sick, because Sally had stood at the door with it, one chilly, damp morning, while she was feeding the chickens; and the eldest girl screaming and screeching at the thoughts of going to bed, because Sally, in order to bring her under her authority, had told her a frightful 'raw-head-and-bloody-bones' story; the horse had broken into the garden, and made wretched work with the vegetables; and fifty pounds of butter had become fit for the grease-pot, because the hoops of the firkin had sprung, and Sally had so much to do, that she never thought of going to see whether the butter was covered with brine.

After six or eight weeks, the children were pretty well restored to orderly habits; and the wife, being really a notable and prudent woman, resolved to make up for her lost butter and vegetables, by doing without help through the winter. When summer came, they should have boarders, she said; and sure enough, they had boarders in plenty; but not profitable ones. There were forty cousins, at whose houses they had stopped; and twenty people who had been very polite to them on the way; and it being such a pleasant season, and *travelling so cheap*, everyone of these people felt they had *a right* to take a journey; and they could not help passing a day or two with their friends at the farm. One after another came, till the farmer could bear it no longer. 'I tell you what, wife,' said he, 'I am going to jail as fast as a man can go. If there is no other way of putting a stop to this, I'll sell every bed in the house, except the one we sleep on.'

And sure enough, he actually did this; and when the forty-first cousin came down on a friendly visit, on account of what her other cousins had told her about the cheapness of travelling, she was told they should be very happy to sleep on the floor, for the sake of accommodating her, for a night or two; but the truth was, they had but one bed in the house. This honest couple are now busy in paying off their debts, and laying by something for their old age. He facetiously tells how he went to New York to have his watch stolen, and his boots blacked like a looking glass; and she shows her Lake George diamond ring, and tells how the steamboat was crowded, and how afraid she was the boiler would burst, and always ends by saying, 'After all, it was a toil of pleasure.'

However, it is not our farmers, who are in the greatest danger of this species of extravagance; for we look to that class of people, as the strongest hold of republican simplicity, industry, and virtue. It is from adventurers, swindlers, broken down traders,—all that rapidly increasing class of idlers, too genteel to work, and too proud to beg,—that we have most reason to dread examples of extravagance. A very respectable tavern-keeper has lately been driven to establish a rule, that no customer shall be allowed to rise from the table till he pays for his meal. 'I know it is rude to give such orders to honest men,' said he, 'and three years ago I would as soon cut off my hand as have done it; but now, travelling is so cheap, that all sorts of characters are on the move; and I find more than half of them will get away, if they can, without paying a cent.'

With regard to public amusements, it is still worse. Rope-dancers, and opera-dancers, and all sorts of dancers, go through the country, making thousands as they go; while, from high to low, there is one universal, despairing groan of 'hard times,' 'dreadful gloomy times!'

161

These things ought not to be. People who have little to spend, should partake sparingly of useless amusements; those who are in debt should deny themselves entirely. Let me not be supposed to inculcate exclusive doctrines. I would have every species of enjoyment as open to the poor as to the rich; but I would have people consider well how they are likely to obtain the greatest portion of happiness, taking the whole of their lives into view; I would not have them sacrifice permanent respectability and comfort to present gentility and love of excitement; above all, I caution them to beware that this love of excitement does not grow into a habit, till the fireside becomes a dull place, and the gambling table and the bar-room finish what the theatre began.

If men would have women economical, they must be so themselves. What motive is there for patient industry, and careful economy, when the savings of a month are spent at one trip to Nahant, and more than the value of a much desired, but rejected dress, is expended during the stay of a new set of comedians? We make a great deal of talk about being republicans; if we are so in reality, we shall stay at home, to mind our business, and educate our children, so long as one or the other need our attention, or can suffer by our neglect.

not rich. Is knowledge the pearl of price in your estimation? That too may be purchased by steady application, and long, solitary hours of study and reflection. "But," says the man of letters, "what a hardship is it that many an illiterate fellow, who cannot construe the motto on his coach, shall raise a fortune, and make a figure, while I possess merely the common conveniences of life." Was it for fortune, then, that you grew pale over the midnight lamp, and gave the sprightly years of youth to study and reflection? You then have mistaken your path, and ill employed your industry. "What reward have I then for all my labor?" What reward! A large comprehensive soul, purged from vulgar fears and prejudices, able to interpret the works of man and God. A perpetual spring of fresh ideas, and the conscious dignity of superior intelligence. Good Heaven! what other reward can you ask! "But is it not a reproach upon the economy of Providence that such a one, who is a mean, dirty fellow, should have amassed wealth enough to buy half a nation?" Not in the least. He made himself a mean, dirty fellow, for that very end. He has paid his health, his conscience, and his liberty for it. Do you envy him his bargain? Will you hang your head in his presence, because he outshines you in equipage and show? Lift up your brow with a noble confidence, and say to yourself, "I have not these things, it is true; but it is because I have not desired, or sought them; it is because I possess something better. I have chosen my lot! I

am content, and satisfied." The most characteristic mark of a
great mind is to choose some one object, which it considers
important, and pursue that object through life. If we expect
the purchase, we must pay the price.'

'There is a pretty passage in one of Lucian's dialogues,
where Jupiter complains to Cupid, that, though he has had
so many intrigues, he was never sincerely beloved. "In order
to be loved," says Cupid, "you must lay aside your aegis and
your thunder-bolts; you must curl and perfume your hair,
and place a garland on your head, and walk with a soft step,
and assume a winning, obsequious deportment." "But,"
replied Jupiter, "I am not willing to resign so much of my
dignity." "Then," returned Cupid, "leave off desiring to be
loved."'

These remarks by Mrs. Barbauld are full of sound
philosophy. Who has not observed, in his circle of
acquaintance, and in the recesses of his own heart, the
same inconsistency of expectation, the same peevishness of
discontent.

Says Germanicus, 'There is my dunce of a classmate has
found his way into Congress, and is living amid the perpetual
excitement of intellectual minds, while I am cooped up in an
ignorant country parish, obliged to be at the beck and call of
every old woman, who happens to feel uneasy in her mind.'

'Well, Germanicus, the road to political distinction was
as open to you as to him; why did you not choose it?' 'Oh,

I could not consent to be the tool of a party; to shake hands with the vicious, and flatter fools. It would gall me to the quick to hear my opponents accuse me of actions I never committed, and of motives which worlds would not tempt me to indulge.' Since Germanicus is wise enough to know the whistle costs more than it is worth, is he not unreasonable to murmur because he has not bought it?

Matrona always wears a discontented look when she hears the praises of Clio. 'I used to write her composition for her, when we were at school together,' says she; 'and now she is quite the idol of the literary world; while I am never heard of beyond my own family, unless some one happens to introduce me as the friend of Clio.' 'Why not write, then; and see if the world will not learn to introduce Clio as the friend of Matrona?' 'I write! not for the world! I could not endure to pour my soul out to an undiscerning multitude; I could not see my cherished thoughts caricatured by some soulless reviewer, and my favorite fancies expounded by the matter-of-fact editor of some stupid paper.' Why does Matrona envy what she knows costs so much, and is of so little value?

Yet so it is, through all classes of society. All of us covet some neighbor's possession, and think our lot would have been happier, had it been different from what it is. Yet most of us could obtain worldly distinctions, if our habits and inclinations allowed us to pay the immense price at which they must be purchased. True wisdom lies in finding out all the advantages of a situation in which we *are* placed, instead of imagining the enjoyments of one in which we are *not* placed.

Such philosophy is rarely found. The most perfect sample I ever met was an old woman, who was apparently the poorest and most forlorn of the human species—so true is the maxim which all profess to believe, and which none act upon invariably, viz. that happiness does not depend on outward circumstances. The wise woman, to whom I have alluded, *walks* to Boston, from a distance of twenty-five or thirty miles, to sell a bag of brown thread and stockings; and then patiently foots it back again with her little gains. Her dress, though tidy, is a grotesque collection of 'shreds and patches,' coarse in the extreme. 'Why don't you come down in a wagon?' said I, when I observed that she was soon to become a mother, and was evidently wearied with her long journey. 'We h'an't got any horse,' replied she; 'the neighbors are very kind to me, but they can't spare their'n; and it would cost as much to hire one, as all my thread will come to.' 'You have a husband—don't he do anything for you.' 'He is a good man; he does all he can; but he's a cripple and an invalid. He reels my yarn, and *specks* the children's shoes. He's as kind a husband as a woman need to have.' 'But his being a cripple is a heavy misfortune to you,' said I. 'Why, ma'am, I don't look upon it in that light,' replied the thread-woman;

'I consider that I've great reason to be thankful he never took to any bad habits.' 'How many children have you?' 'Six sons, and five *darters*, ma'am.' 'Six sons and five daughters! What a family for a poor woman to support!' 'It's a family, surely, ma'am; but there an't one of 'em I'd be willing to lose. They are as good children as need to be—all willing to work, and all clever to me. Even the littlest boy, when he gets a cent now and then for doing a *chore*, will be sure and bring it to ma'am.' 'Do your daughters spin your thread?' 'No, ma'am; as soon as they are old enough, they go out to *sarvice*. I don't want to keep them always delving for me; they are always willing to give me what they can; but it is right and fair they should do a little for themselves. I do all my spinning after the folks are abed.' 'Don't you think you should be better off, if you had no one but yourself to provide for?' 'Why, no, ma'am, I don't. If I hadn't been married, I should always have had to work as hard as I could; and now I can't do more than that. My children are a great comfort to me; and I look forward to the time when they'll do as much for me as I have done for them.'

Here was true philosophy! I learned a lesson from that poor woman which I shall not soon forget. If I wanted true, hearty, well principled service, I would employ children brought up by such a mother.

REASONS FOR HARD TIMES.

Perhaps there never was a time when the depressing effects of stagnation in business were so universally felt, all the world over, as they are now.—The merchant sends out old dollars, and is lucky if he gets the same number of new ones in return; and he who has a share in manufactures, has bought a 'bottle imp,' which he will do well to hawk about the street for the lowest possible coin. The effects of this depression must of course be felt by all grades of society. Yet who that passes through Cornhill at one o'clock, and sees the bright array of wives and daughters, as various in their decorations as the insects, the birds and the shells, would believe that the community was staggering under a weight which almost paralyzes its movements? 'Everything is so cheap,' say the ladies, 'that it is inexcusable not to dress well.' But do they reflect *why* things are so cheap? Do they know how much wealth has been sacrificed, how many families ruined, to produce this boasted result? Do they not know enough of the machinery of society, to suppose that the stunning effect of crash after crash, may eventually be felt by those on whom they depend for support?

Luxuries are cheaper now than necessaries were a few years since; yet it is a lamentable fact, that it costs more to live now than it did formerly. When silk was nine shillings per yard, seven or eight yards sufficed for a dress; now it is four or five shillings, sixteen or twenty yards will hardly satisfy the mantuamaker.

If this extravagance were confined to the wealthiest classes, it would be productive of more good than evil. But if the rich have a new dress every fortnight, people of moderate fortune will have one every month. In this way, finery becomes the standard of respectability; and a man's cloth is of more consequence than his character.

Men of fixed salaries spend every cent of their income, and then leave their children to depend on the precarious charity and reluctant friendship of a world they have wasted their substance to please. Men who rush into enterprise and speculation, keep up their credit by splendor; and should they sink, they and their families carry with them extravagant habits to corrode their spirits with discontent, perchance to tempt them into crime. 'I know we are extravagant,' said one of my acquaintance, the other day; 'but how can I help it? My husband does not like to see his wife and daughters dress more meanly than those with whom they associate.' 'Then, my dear lady, your husband has not as much moral dignity and moral courage as I thought he had. He should be content to see his wife and daughters respected for neatness, good taste, and attractive manners.' 'This all sounds very well in talk,' replied the lady; 'but, say what you will about pleasing and intelligent girls, nobody will attend to them unless they dress in the fashion. If my daughters were to dress in the plain, neat style you recommend, they would see all their acquaintance asked to dance more frequently than themselves, and not a gentleman would join them in Cornhill.'

'I do not believe this in so extensive a sense as you do. Girls may appear genteelly without being extravagant, and though some fops may know the most approved color for a ribbon, or the newest arrangement for trimming, I believe gentlemen of real character merely notice whether a lady's dress is generally in good taste, or not. But, granting your statement to be true, in its widest sense, of what consequence is it? How much will the whole happiness of your daughter's life be affected by her dancing some fifty times less than her companions, or wasting some few hours less in the empty conversation of coxcombs? A man often admires a style of dress, which he would not venture to support in a wife. Extravagance has prevented many marriages, and rendered still more unhappy. And should your daughters fail in forming good connexions, what have you to leave them, save extravagant habits, too deeply rooted to be eradicated. Think you those who now laugh at them for a soiled glove, or an unfashionable ribbon, will assist their poverty, or cheer their neglected old age? No; they would find them as cold and selfish as they are vain. A few thousands in the bank are worth all the fashionable friends in Christendom.'

Whether my friend was convinced, or not, I cannot say; but I saw her daughters in Cornhill, the next week, with new French hats and blonde veils.

It is really melancholy to see how this fever of extravagance rages, and how it is sapping the strength of our happy country. It has no bounds; it pervades all ranks, and characterizes all ages.

I know the wife of a pavier, who spends her three hundred a year in 'outward adorning,' and who will not condescend to speak to her husband, while engaged in his honest calling.

Mechanics, who should have too high a sense of their own respectability to resort to such pitiful competition, will indulge their daughters in dressing like the wealthiest; and a domestic would certainly leave you, should you dare advise her to lay up one cent of her wages.

'These things ought not to be.' Every man and every woman should lay up some portion of their income, whether that income be great or small.

and what inordinate importance they learned to attach to them, when they heard them constantly talked about.

In his family, Sunday was a happy day; for it was made a day of religious instruction, without any unnatural constraint upon the gayety of the young. The Bible was the text book; the places mentioned in it were traced on maps; the manners and customs of different nations were explained; curious phenomena in the natural history of those countries were read; in a word, everything was done to cherish a spirit of humble, yet earnest inquiry. In this excellent family Mrs. —— remained till her marriage. In the course of fifteen years, she lost her uncle, her aunt, and her husband. She was left destitute, but supported herself comfortably by her own exertions, and retained the respect and admiration of a large circle of friends. Thus she passed her life in cheerfulness and honor during ten years; at the end of that time, her humble residence took fire from an adjoining house in the night time, and she escaped by jumping from the chamber window. In consequence of the injury received by this fall, her right arm was amputated, and her right leg became entirely useless. Her friends were very kind and attentive; and for a short time she consented to live on their bounty; but, aware that the claims on private charity are very numerous, she, with the genuine independence of a strong mind, resolved to avail herself of the public provision for the helpless poor. The name of going to the alms-house had nothing terrifying

174

or disgraceful to *her*; for she had been taught that *conduct* is the real standard of respectability. She is there, with a heart full of thankfulness to the Giver of all things; she is patient, pious, and uniformly cheerful. She instructs the young, encourages the old, and makes herself delightful to all, by her various knowledge and entertaining conversation. Her character reflects dignity on her situation; and those who visit the establishment, come away with sentiments of respect and admiration for this voluntary resident of the alms-house.

What a contrast is afforded by the character of the woman who occupies the room next hers! She is so indolent and filthy, that she can with difficulty be made to attend to her own personal comfort; and even the most patient are worn out with her perpetual fretfulness. Her mind is continually infested with envy, hatred, and discontent She thinks Providence has dealt hardly with her; that all the world are proud and ungrateful; and that every one despises her because she is in the alms-house. This pitiable state of mind is the natural result of her education.

Her father was a respectable mechanic, and might have been a wealthy one, had he not been fascinated by the beauty of a thoughtless, idle, showy girl, whom he made his wife. The usual consequences followed—he could not earn money so fast as she could spend it; the house became a scene of discord; the daughter dressed in the fashion; learned to play on the piano; was taught to think that being engaged in any useful employment was very ungenteel; and that to be *engaged to be married* was the chief end and aim of woman; the father died a bankrupt; the weak and frivolous mother lingered along in beggary, for a while, and then died of vexation and shame.

The friends of the family were very kind to the daughter; but her extreme indolence, her vanity, pertness, and ingratitude, finally exhausted the kindness of the most generous and forbearing; and as nothing could induce her to personal exertion, she was at length obliged to take shelter in the alms-house. Here her misery is incurable. She has so long been accustomed to think dress and parade the necessary elements of happiness, that she despises all that is done for her comfort; her face has settled into an expression which looks like an imbodied growl; every body is tired of listening to her complaints; and even the little children run away, when they see her coming.

May not those who have children to educate, learn a good lesson from these women? Those who have wealth, have recently had many and bitter lessons to prove how suddenly riches may take to themselves wings; and those who *certainly* have but little to leave, should indeed beware how they bestow upon their children, the accursed inheritance of indolent and extravagant habits.

APPENDIX

TO THE
AMERICAN FRUGAL HOUSEWIFE.

Those sentences marked with a star relate to subjects mentioned in other parts of the book.

To PRESERVE GREEN CURRANTS.—Currants maybe kept fresh for a year or more, if they are gathered when green, separated from the stems, put into dry, clean junk bottles, and corked very carefully, so as to exclude the air. They should be kept in a cool place in the cellar.

CANDLES.—Very hard and durable candles are made in the following manner: Melt together ten ounces of mutton tallow, a quarter of an ounce of camphor, four ounces of beeswax, and two ounces of alum. Candles made of these materials burn with a very clear light.

*VARNISHED FURNITURE.—If you wish to give a fine soft polish to varnished furniture, and remove any slight imperfections, rub it once or twice a week with pulverized rotten-stone and linseed oil, and afterward wipe clean with a soft silk rag.

CREAM.—The quantity of cream on milk may be greatly increased by the following process: Have two pans ready in boiling hot water, and when the new milk is brought in, put it into one of these hot pans and cover it with the other. The quality as well as the thickness of the cream is improved.

*TEETH.—Honey mixed with pure pulverized charcoal is said to be excellent to cleanse the teeth, and make them white. Lime-water with a little Peruvian bark is very good to be occasionally used by those who have defective teeth, or an offensive breath.

TAINTED BUTTER.—Some good cooks say that bad butter may be purified in the following manner: Melt and skim it, then put into it a piece of *well-toasted* bread; in a few minutes the butter will lose its offensive taste and smell; the bread will absorb it all. Slices of potato fried in rancid lard will in a great measure absorb the unpleasant taste.

TOMATOES PIE.—Tomatoes make excellent pies. Skins taken off with scalding water, stewed twenty minutes or more, salted, prepared the same as rich squash pies, only an egg or two more.

*It is a great improvement to the flavor of PUMPKIN PIES to boil the milk, stir the sifted pumpkin into it, and let them boil up together once or twice. The pumpkin swells almost as much as Indian meal, and of course absorbs more milk than when stirred together cold; but the taste of the pie is much improved.

Some people cut pumpkin, string it, and dry it like apples. It is a much better way to boil and sift the pumpkin, then spread it out thin in tin plates, and dry hard in a warm oven. It will keep good all the year round, and a little piece boiled up in milk will make a batch of pies.

*Most people think BRASS KETTLES for washing are not as likely to collect verdigris, if they are never cleaned in any other way than by washing in strong soap suds just before they are used.

INK SPOTS.—If soaked in warm milk before the ink has a chance to dry, the spot may usually be removed. If it has dried in, rub table-salt upon it, and drop lemon-juice upon the salt. This answers nearly as well as the salts of lemon sold by apothecaries. If a lemon cannot be easily procured, vinegar, or sorrel-juice, will answer. White soap diluted with vinegar is likewise a good thing to take out ink spots.

STARCH.—Frozen potatoes yield more flour for starch than fresh ones. The frost may be taken out by soaking them in cold water a few hours before cooking; if frozen very hard, it may be useful to throw a little saltpetre into the water.

FEATHERS.—It is said that tumbled plumes may be restored to elasticity and beauty by dipping them in hot water, then shaking and drying them.

ICY STEPS.—Salt strewed upon the door-steps in winter will cause the ice to crack, so that it can be easily removed.

FLOWERS.—Flowers may be preserved fresh in tumblers or vases by putting a handful of salt in the water, to increase its coldness.

WHITE-WASHING is said to last longer if the new-slaked lime be mixed with skim-milk.

HORSE-FLIES.—Indigo-weed stuck plentifully about the harness tends to keep flies from horses. Some make a decoction of indigo-weed, and others of pennyroyal, and bathe horses with it, to defend them from insects.

PINE APPLES will keep much better if the green crown at top be twisted off. The vegetation of the crown takes the goodness from the fruit, in the same way that sprouts injure vegetables. The crown can be stuck on for ornament, if necessary.

*THE PILES.—Those who have tried other remedies for this disorder in vain, have found relief from the following medicine: Stew a handful of low mallows in about three gills of milk; strain it, and mix about half the quantity of West India molasses with it. As warm as is agreeable.

WARTS.—It is said that if the top of a wart be wet and rubbed two or three times a day with a piece of unslaked lime, it cures the wart soon, and leaves no scar.

*CANCERS.—The Indians have great belief in the efficacy of poultices of stewed cranberries, for the relief of *cancers*. They apply them fresh and warm every ten or fifteen minutes, night and day. Whether this will effect a cure I know not; I simply know that the Indians strongly recommend it. Salts, or some simple physic, is taken every day during the process.

EAR-WAX.—Nothing is better than ear-wax to prevent the painful effects resulting from a wound by a nail, skewer, &c. It should be put on as soon as possible. Those who are troubled with cracked lips have found this remedy successful when others have failed. It is one of those sorts of cures, which are very likely to be laughed at; but I know of its having produced very beneficial results.

*BURNS.—If a person who is burned will *patiently* hold the injured part in water, it will prevent the formation of a blister. If the water be too cold, it may be slightly warmed, and produce the same effect. People in general are not willing to try it for a sufficiently long time. Chalk and hog's lard simmered together are said to make a good ointment for a burn.

*BRUISES.—Constant application of warm water is very soothing to bruised flesh, and may serve to prevent bad consequences while other things are in preparation.

SORE NIPPLES.—Put twenty grains of sugar of lead into a vial with one gill of rose-water; shake it up thoroughly;

wet a piece of soft linen with this preparation, and put it on; renew this as often as the linen becomes dry. Before nursing, wash this off with something soothing; rose-water is very good; but the best thing is quince-seed warmed in a little cold tea until the liquid becomes quite glutinous. This application is alike healing and pleasant.

A raw onion is an excellent remedy for the STING OF A WASP.

CORNS.—A corn may be extracted from the foot by binding on half a raw cranberry, with the cut side of the fruit upon the foot. I have known a very old and troublesome corn drawn out in this way, in the course of a few nights.

HEART-BURN.—Eat magnesia for the heart-burn.

CHLORIDE OF LIME.—A room may be purified from offensive smells of any kind by a few spoonsful of chloride of lime dissolved in water. A good-sized saucer, or some similar vessel, is large enough for all common purposes. The article is cheap, and is invaluable in the apartment of an invalid.

EGGS IN WINTER.—The reason hens do not usually lay eggs in the winter is that the gravel is covered up with snow, and therefore they are not furnished with lime to form the shells. If the bones left of meat, poultry, &c. are pounded and mixed with their food, or given to them alone, they will eat them very eagerly, and will lay eggs the same as in summer. Hens fed on oats are much more likely to lay well than those fed on corn.

PEARLS.—In order to preserve the beauty of pearl ornaments, they should be carefully kept from dampness. A piece of paper torn off and rolled up, so as to present a soft, ragged edge, is the best thing to cleanse them with.

VARNISHING GILDED FRAMES.—It is said that looking-glass frames may be cleansed with a damp cloth, without injury, provided they are varnished with the *pure white alcoholic varnish*, used for transferred engravings and other delicate articles of fancy-work. This would save the trouble of covering and uncovering picture-frames with the change of the seasons. I never heard how many coats of varnish were necessary, but I should think it would be safe to put on more than one.

COLOGNE WATER.—One pint of alcohol, sixty drops of lavender, sixty drops of bergamot, sixty drops of essence of lemon, sixty drops of orange water. To be corked up, and well shaken. It is better for considerable age.

GREASE SPOTS.—Magnesia rubbed upon the spot, covered with clean paper, and a warm iron placed above, will usually draw out grease. Where a considerable quantity of oil has been spilled, it will be necessary to repeat the operation a great many times, in order to extract it all.

RECEIPT FOR MAKING EXCELLENT BREAD WITHOUT YEAST.—Scald about two handsful of Indian meal, into which put a little salt, and as much cold water as will make it rather warmer than new milk; then stir in wheat flour, till it is as thick as a family pudding, and set it down by the fire to rise. In about half an hour, it generally grows thin; you may sprinkle a little fresh flour on the top, and mind to turn the pot round, that it may not bake to the side of it. In three or four hours, if you mind the above directions, it will rise and ferment as if you had set it with hop yeast; when it does, make it up in soft dough, flour a pan, put in your bread, set it before the fire, covered up, turn it round to make it equally warm, and in about half an hour it will be light enough to bake. It suits best to bake in a Dutch oven, as it should be put into the oven as soon as it is light.

RICE JELLY.—Boil a quarter of a pound of rice flour with half a pound of loaf sugar, in a quart of water, till the whole becomes one glutinous mass, then strain off the jelly and let it stand to cool. This food is very nourishing and beneficial to invalids.

APPLE MARMALADE.—Scald apples till they will pulp from the core; take an equal weight of sugar in large lumps, and boil it in just water enough to dip the lumps well, until it can be skimmed, and is a thick syrup; mix this with the apple pulp, and simmer it on a quick fire for fifteen minutes. Keep it in pots covered with paper dipped in brandy.

QUINCE MARMALADE.—To two pounds of quince put three quarters of a pound of nice sugar, and a pint of spring water. Boil them till they are tender; then take them up and bruise them; again put them in the liquor, and let them boil three quarters of an hour, then put it into jars, covered as mentioned above. Those who like things very sweet put an equal quantity of quince and sugar; but I think the flavor is less delicious.

RASPBERRY JAM.—Take an equal quantity of fruit and sugar. Put the raspberries into a pan, boil and stir them constantly till juicy and well broken; add as much sugar, boil and skim it till it is reduced to a fine jam. Put it away in the same manner as other preserves.

BLANC-MANGER.—Boil two ounces of isinglass in one pint and a half of new milk; strain it into one pint of thick cream. Sweeten it to your taste, add one cup of rose-water, boil it up once, let it settle, and put it in your moulds.

Some prefer to boil two ounces of isinglass in three and a half pints of water for half an hour, then strain it to one pint and a half of cream, sweeten it, add a teacup of rose-water, and boil up once.

Isinglass is the most expensive ingredient in blanc-manger. Some decidedly prefer the jelly of calves' feet. The jelly is obtained by boiling four feet in a gallon of water till reduced to a quart, strained, cooled, and skimmed. A pint of jelly to a pint of cream; in other respects done the same as isinglass blanc-manger. Some boil a stick of cinnamon, or a grated lemon-peel, in the jelly. The moulds should be made thoroughly clean, and wet with cold water; the white of an egg, dropped in and shook round the moulds, will make it come out smooth and handsomely.

PORK JELLY.—Some people like the jelly obtained from a boiled hand of pork, or the feet of pork, prepared in the same way as calf's-foot jelly; for which see page 31.

The cloths, or jelly-bags, through which jelly is strained, should be first wet to prevent waste.

CRANBERRY JELLY.—Mix isinglass jelly, or calf's-foot jelly, with a double quantity of cranberry juice, sweeten it with fine loaf sugar, boil it up once, and strain it to cool.

RICH CUSTARDS.—Boil a pint of milk with lemon-peel and a stick of cinnamon. While it is boiling, beat up the yolks of five eggs with a pint of cream. When the milk tastes of the spice, pour it to the cream, stirring well; sweeten it to taste. Give the custard a simmer, till of a proper thickness, but do not let it boil. Stir the whole time one way. Season it with a little rose-water, and a few spoonsful of wine or brandy, as you may prefer. When put into cups, grate on nutmeg.

TO PRESERVE PEACHES.—Scald peaches in boiling water, but do not let them boil; take them out and put them in cold water, then dry them in a sieve, and put them in long, wide-mouthed bottles. To a half dozen peaches put a quarter of a pound of clarified sugar; pour it over the peaches, fill up the bottles with brandy, and stop them close.

COCOA-NUT CAKES.—Grate the meat of two cocoa-nuts, after pealing off the dark skin; allow an equal weight of loaf sugar, pounded and sifted, and the rind and juice of two lemons. Mix the ingredients well; make into cakes about as big as a nutmeg, with a little piece of citron in each. Bake them on buttered tin sheets about twenty minutes, in a moderately hot oven.

*TO CLARIFY SUGAR.—Put half a pint of water to a pound of sugar; whip up the white of an egg and stir it in, and put it over the fire. When it first boils up, check it with a little cold water; the second time set it away to cool. In a quarter of an hour, skim the top, and turn the syrup off quickly, so as to leave the sediment which will collect at the bottom.

*RICH WEDDING CAKE.—One pound three quarters of flour, one pound one quarter of butter, do. of sugar, one dozen eggs, two pounds of currants, one gill of wine, half a gill of brandy, one pound of citron, cut in slices, a wine-glass of rose-water, three quarters of an ounce of nutmeg, quarter of an ounce of cloves, the same of allspice. The rind of two lemons grated in. See page 72 for baking.

STILL RICHER WEDDING CAKE.—Three pounds of flour, three pounds of butter, three pounds of sugar, twenty-eight eggs, six pounds of currants, and six pounds of seeded raisins; one ounce of cinnamon, one ounce of nutmeg, three quarters of an ounce of cloves, half an ounce of mace, one pound of citron, two glasses of brandy, two glasses of rose-water, and one glass of wine. For baking, see page 72.

*FROSTING FOR CAKE.—It is a great improvement to squeeze a little lemon-juice into the egg and sugar prepared for frosting. It gives a fine flavor, and makes it extremely white. For frosting, see directions, page 72.

WHIP SYLLABUB.—One pint of cream, one pint of wine, the juice and grated peel of a lemon, and the white of two eggs; sweeten it to your taste, put it into a deep vessel, and whip it to a light froth. Fill your glasses with the froth as it rises. It is a good plan to put some of the froth in a sieve, over a dish, and have it in readiness to heap upon the top of your glasses after you have filled them. Some people put a spoonful of marmalade or jelly at the bottom of the glasses, before they are filled.

LOBSTER SALAD.—The meat of one lobster is extracted from the shell, and cut up fine. Have fresh hard lettuce cut up very fine; mix it with the lobster. Make a dressing, in a deep plate, of the yolks of four eggs cut up, a gill of sweet oil, a gill of vinegar, half a gill of mustard, half a teaspoonful of cayenne, half a teaspoonful of salt; all mixed well together. To be prepared just before eaten. Chicken salad is prepared in the same way, only chicken is used instead of lobster, and celery instead of lettuce.

ESCALOPED OYSTERS.—Put crumbled bread around the sides and bottom of a buttered dish. Put oysters in a skillet, and let the heat just strike them through; then take them out of the shells, and rinse them thoroughly in the water they have stewed in. Put half of them on the layer of crumbled bread, and season with mace and pepper; cover them with crumbs of bread and bits of butter; put in the rest of the oysters, season and cover them in the same way. Strain their liquor, and pour over. If you fear they will be too salt, put fresh water instead. Bake fifteen or twenty minutes.

FRIED OYSTERS.—After they are prepared from the shell, they are dipped in batter, made of eggs and crumbs, seasoned with nutmeg, mace and salt, stirred up well. Fried in lard till brown.

VEGETABLE OYSTER.—This vegetable is something like a parsnip; is planted about the same time, ripens about the same time, and requires about the same cooking. It is said to taste very much like real oysters. It is cut in pieces, after being boiled, dipped in batter, and fried in the same way. It is excellent mixed with minced salt fish.

PARTRIDGES should be roasted ten or fifteen minutes longer than chickens, that is, provided they are thick-breasted and plump. Being naturally dry, they should be plentifully basted with butter.

EXTRACTS FROM THE ***ENGLISH*** FRUGAL HOUSEWIFE.

[It was the intention of the author of the *American Frugal Housewife*, to have given an Appendix from the *English* Frugal Housewife; but upon examination, she found the book so little fitted to the wants of this country, that she has been able to extract but little.]

CHEESE is to be chosen by its moist, smooth coat; if old cheese be rough-coated, ragged, or dry at top, beware of worms. If it be over-full of holes, moist and spongy, it is subject to maggots. If soft or perished places appear, try how deep they go, for the worst part may be hidden.

EGGS.—To prove whether they are good or bad, hold the large end of the egg to your tongue; if it feels warm, it is new; but if cold, it is bad. In proportion to the heat or cold, is the goodness of the egg. Another way to know is to put the egg in a pan of cold water; the fresher the egg, the sooner it will fall to the bottom; if rotten, it will swim. If you keep your eggs in ashes, salt or bran, put the small end downwards; if you turn them endways once a week, they will keep some months.

VEAL.—If the vein in the shoulder look blue or bright red, it is newly killed; but if black, green, or yellow, it is stale. The leg is known to be new by the stiffness of the joint. The head of a calf or a lamb is known by the eyes; if sunk or wrinkled, it is stale; if plump and lively, it is fresh.

MUTTON.—If it be young, the flesh will pinch tender; if old, it will wrinkle and remain so. If young, the fat will easily part from the lean; if old, it will stick by strings and skins. Strong, rancid mutton feels spongy, and does not rise again easily, when dented. The flesh of ewe mutton is paler, of a closer grain, and parts more easily.

BEEF.—Good beef has an open grain, and a tender, oily smoothness; a pleasant carnation color, and clear white suet, betoken good meat; yellow suet is not so good.

PORK.—If young, the lean will break in pinching, and if you nip the skin with your nails, it will make a dent; the fat will be soft and pulpy, like lard. If the lean be tough, and the fat flabby and spongy, feeling rough, it is old, especially if the rind be stubborn, and you cannot nip it with your nails. Little kernels, like nail-shot, in the fat, are a sign that it is measly, and dangerous to be eaten.

CARVING.

[Written for the *American* Frugal Housewife.]
TO CARVE A TURKEY.—Fix the fork firmly on one side of the thin bone that rises in the centre of the breast; the fork should be placed *parallel* with the bone, and as close to it as possible. Cut the meat from the breast lengthwise, in slices of about half an inch in thickness. Then turn the turkey upon the side nearest you, and cut off the leg and the wing; when the knife is passed between the limbs and the body, and pressed outward, the joint will be easily perceived. Then turn the turkey on the other side, and cut off the other leg and wing. Separate the drum-sticks from the leg-bones, and the pinions from the wings; it is hardly possible to mistake the joint. Cut the stuffing in thin slices, lengthwise. Take off the neck-bones, which are two triangular bones on each side of the breast; this is done by passing the knife from the back under the blade-part of each neck-bone, until it reaches the end; by raising the knife, the other branch will easily crack off. Separate the carcass from the back by passing the knife lengthwise from the neck downward. Turn the back upwards, and lay the edge of the knife across the back-bone, about midway between the legs and wings; at the same moment, place the fork within the lower part of the turkey, and lift it up; this will make the back-bone crack

at the knife. The croup, or lower part of the back, being cut off, put it on the plate, with the rump from you, and split off the side-bones by forcing the knife through from the rump to the other end.

The choicest parts of a turkey are the side-bones, the breast, and the thigh-bones. The breast and wings are called light meat; the thigh-bones and side-bones dark meat. When a person declines expressing a preference, it is polite to help to both kinds.

A SIRLOIN OF BEEF.—Place the curving bone downward upon the dish. Cut the outside lengthwise, separating *each slice* from the chine-bone, with the point of the knife. Some people cut through at the chine, slip the knife under, and cut the meat out in one mass, which they afterward cut in slices; but this is not the best, or the most proper way. The tender loin is on the inside; it is to be cut crosswise.

A HAM.—Begin in the middle of a ham; cut across the bone, and take thin slices from either side.

A GOOSE.—A goose is carved nearly as a turkey, only the breast should be cut in slices narrow and nearly square, instead of broad, like that of turkey; and before passing the knife to separate the legs and wings, the fork is to be placed in the small end of the leg-bone or pinion, and the part pressed close to the body, when the separation will be easy. Take off the merrythought, the neck-bones, and separate the leg-bones from the legs, and the pinions from the wings. The best parts are the breast, the thigh-bones, and the fleshy parts of the wings.

A PIG.—If the pig be whole, cut off the head, and split it in halves along the back-bone. Separate the shoulders and legs by passing the knife under them in a circular direction. The best parts are the triangular piece of the neck, the ribs, legs and shoulders.

A FILLET OF VEAL.—This is the thick part of the leg, and is to be cut smooth, round and close to the bone. Some prefer the outside piece. A little fat cut from the skirt is to be served to each plate.

MUTTON.—A saddle of mutton is the two loins together, and the back-bone running down the middle to the tail. Slices are to be cut out parallel to the back-bone on either side.

In a leg of mutton, the knife is to be entered in the thick fleshy part, as near the shank as will give a good slice. Cut towards the large end, and always to the bone.

Footnote 1:

There are two kinds of green paint; one is of no use in destroying insects.

Footnote 2:

Some think it an improvement to make whey of vinegar and milk, and heat it well up with the eggs before the lime is put in. I have heard of iron mended with it.

Footnote 3:

Among the numerous medicines for this disease, perhaps none, after all, is better, particularly where the bowels are inflamed, than the old-fashioned one of English-mallows steeped in milk, and drank freely. Everybody knows, of course, that English-mallows and marsh-mallows are different herbs.

Footnote 4:

This plant resembles the poisonous kill-lamb, both in the shape and the glossiness of the leaves: great care should be used to distinguish them.

Made in the USA
San Bernardino, CA
11 February 2016